中华五福

Designs of Chinese Blessings

Wealth

主　编／黄全信

副主编／黄迎　李　进

编　委／吴曼丽　任晋英　沈世通　江　燕　严学佳

朱　迪　彭　荣　高　明　洪育强

翻　译／李迎春

华语教学出版社
SINOLINGUA

First Edition 2003

ISBN 7-80052-893-6

Published by Sinolingua
24 Baiwanzhuang Road, Beijing 100037, China
Tel: (86) 10-68995871/68326333
Fax: (86) 10-68326333
E-mail: hyjx @263.net
Printed by Beijing Foreign Languages Printing House
Distributed by China International
Book Trading Corporation
35 Chegongzhuang Xilu, P.O.Box 399
Beijing 100044, China

Printed in the People's Republic of China

喜
進
財
添
目录
contents

176/ 钱龙引进

Fortune introduced by the dragon of coins

178/ 钱龙引进

Fortune introduced by the dragon of coins

180/ 淂利图

The picture of gains

182/ 家家淂利

Gains to all households

184/ 黄金万两

10,000 ounces of gold

186/ 推车进宝

Pushing over the cart to present treasure

188/ 推车进宝

Pushing over the cart to present treasure

190/ 推车进宝

Pushing over the cart to present treasure

192/ 推车进宝

Pushing over the cart to present treasure

194/ 常富贵

Wealth and rank at all times

196/ 累积资金

Capital accumulation

198/ 添财进喜

Fortune added is happiness increased

200/ 添财进喜

Fortune added is happiness increased

202/ 渔翁淂利

The fisherman has the gains

人臻五福　花满三春

吉祥一词，始见于《易经》："吉事有祥。"《左传》有："是何祥也？吉祥焉在？"《庄子》则有："虚室生日，吉祥止止。"《注疏》云："吉者，福善之事；祥者，嘉庆之征。"

吉祥二字，在甲骨文中被写作"吉羊"。上古人过着游牧生活，羊肥大成群是很"吉祥"的事，在古器物的铭文中多有"吉羊"。《说文》云："羊，祥也。"

吉祥，是美好、幸运的形象；吉祥，是人类最迷人的主题。艺术，最终都是把理想形象化；吉祥图，是中华吉祥文化最璀璨的明珠。旧时有联："善果皆欢喜，香云普吉祥。"吉祥图有：吉祥如意、五福吉祥等。

五福，是吉祥的具体。福、禄、寿、喜、财，在民间被称为五福；福星、禄星、寿星、喜神、财神，在仙界被尊为五福神。五福最早见于《尚书》："五福：一曰寿，二曰富，三曰

康宁，四曰攸好德，五曰考终命。”旧时有联：“三阳临吉地，五福萃华门。”吉祥图有：五福捧寿、三多五福等。

福，意为幸福美满。《老子》：“福兮，祸所伏。”《韩非子》：“全富贵之谓福。”旧时有联：“香焚一炷，福赐三多。”吉祥图有：福在眼前、纳福迎祥、翘盼福音、天官赐福等。

禄，意为高官厚禄。《左传》：“介之推不言禄，禄亦弗及。”《汉书》：“身宠而载高位，家温而食厚禄。”旧时有联：“同科十进士，庆榜三名元。”吉祥图有：禄位高升、福禄寿禧、天赐禄爵、加官进禄等。

寿，意为健康长寿。《庄子》：“人，上寿百岁，中寿八十，下寿六十。”《诗经》：“如南山之寿，不骞不崩。”旧时有联：“同臻寿域，共跻春台。”吉祥图有：寿星高照、鹤寿千年、富贵寿考、蟠桃献寿等。

喜，意为欢乐喜庆。《国语》：“固庆其喜而吊其忧。”韦昭注：“喜犹福也。”旧时有联：“笑到几时方合口，坐来无日不开怀。”吉祥图有：喜上眉梢、双喜临门、端阳喜庆、皆大欢喜等。

财，意为发财富有。《荀子》：“务本节用财无极。”旧时有联：“生意兴隆通四海，财源茂盛达三江。”吉祥图有：财源滚滚、招财进宝、喜交财运、升官发财等。

吉祥图，不仅有“五福”之内涵，而且是

绘画艺术和语言艺术的珠联璧合。在绘画上，体现了中国画主要的表现手段——线的魅力，给人以美感，令人赏心悦目。吉祥图虽多出自民间画工之手，却多有顾恺之“春蚕吐丝”之韵，曹仲达“曹衣出水”之美，吴道子“吴带当风”之妙；在语言上，通俗和普及了古代文化，吉祥图多配有一句浓缩成四个字的吉语祥词，给人以吉祥，令人心驰神往。

《中华五福吉祥图典》，汇集了我数代家传和几十年收藏的精品吉祥图，可谓美不胜收。其中既有明之典雅，又有清之华丽；既有皇家之富贵，又有民间之纯朴；既有北方之粗犷，又有南方之秀美……按五福全书分成福、禄、寿、喜、财五集，每集吉祥图 119 幅，共 595 幅。除同类图案外，均按笔画顺序编排。基本包括了中国传统吉祥图的各个方面，并对每幅图作了考证和诠释，使之图文并茂，相得益彰。

五福人人喜，吉祥家家乐。吉祥图是中国的，也是世界的，故以汉英对照出版。《中华五福吉祥图典》会给您带来吉祥，给您全家带来幸福。

黄全信于佩实斋

2003 年 1 月 1 日

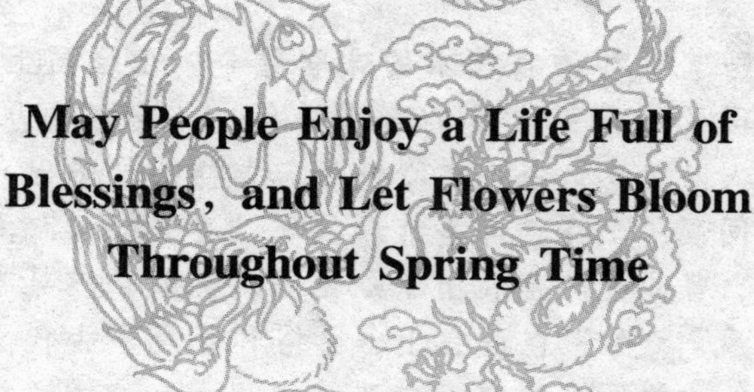

May People Enjoy a Life Full of Blessings, and Let Flowers Bloom Throughout Spring Time

The word jixiang (meaning lucky, propitious, or auspicious) is mentioned in Chinese ancient books and writings as early as in the Zhou Dynasty.

The word jixiang was written as jiyang (lucky sheep) on oracle bones. To the ancient Chinese, who led a nomadic life, large herds of well-fed sheep were auspicious things, and the word jiyang also appeared in engravings on ancient utensils.

To have good luck is mankind's eternal desire. While art records man's ideals, good luck pictures are the most brilliant part of the Chinese good luck culture. An old couplet says that kindness leads to happiness and good luck. Typical good luck pictures are: good luck and heart's content, good luck with five blessings, etc.

The five blessings – good fortune, high salary and a good career, longevity, happiness, and wealth – are the concrete forms of good luck , and there are five kinds of gods presiding over these blessings. The five blessings as they are first mentioned in Chinese literature are not quite the same as the five which are talked about today, though they are quite similar. An old couplet says that as the land of good luck bathes in the Sun, a prosperous family is granted all the blessings. Typical good luck pictures are: long-term enjoyment of all five blessings, more blessings, etc.

Good fortune means happiness and complete satisfaction. Ancient Chinese philosophers, including Lao Zi, all commented on the notion of good fortune. An old couplet says to burn incense to beg for more blessings. Good luck pictures in this theme include good fortune for today, blessings from above, etc.

High salary means handsome salaries at prestigious posts. In old times, Chinese attached great significance to academic excellence, which led in turn to high positions in government. An old couplet says may you distinguish yourselves in the royal examinations and rank at the top of the list. Good luck pictures in this theme used in this book include big improvements in salary and post, salary and position bestowed from heaven, etc.

Longevity refers to good health and a long life. As Zhuangzhou said, and the *Book of Songs* records, longevity is the universal wish of mankind. As wished in an old couplet, to grow to a long life together is a joyful experience. This book has the following good luck pic -

tures concerning longevity: high above shines the star of longevity, live to be 1, 000 years with white hair, and offer the flat peach to wish for longevity, etc.

Happiness refers to happy events and celebrations. Happy events should be celebrated, while those with worries should be consoled according to ancient Chinese literature. An old Chinese couplet says, why not keep on laughing as all days are filled with happiness. Good luck pictures on this theme included in this book include double happiness visits at the door, all's well that ends well, etc.

Wealth means getting rich and having plentiful things. Ancient Chinese believed that the secret to endless wealth is to be down-to-earth and prudent. Illustrating the concept of wealth is an old couplet: a prosperous business deals with people from all corners of the world, and wealth rolls in from afar. Typical good luck pictures of this type include in comes wealth, get rich and win high positions, etc.

Good luck pictures not only incorporate the five blessings but the art of painting and language as well. The beautiful lines of these pictures, done in the style of traditional Chinese painting, provide the viewers with artistic enjoyment which is pleasing to the eyes and heart. Though mostly the work of folk artists, they exhibit a level of craftsmanship worthy of the great and famous masters . The language adopted in these pictures serves to popularize ancient culture, and the four-character good luck phrase accompanying almost every picture depicts an attractive scene.

Designs of Chinese Blessings is a compilation of special good luck pictures passed down in my family for several generations as well those which I have been collecting for dozens of years. Their beauty is beyond description. They combine the elegance of the Ming Dynasty and the magnificence of the Qing Dynasty, the nobility of the royal family and the modesty of the common people, the boldness of the north and the delicacy of the south. The book consists of five sections: good fortune, high salary and a good career, longevity, happiness, and wealth. With 119 pictures in each section, the whole book contains 595 pictures and is a complete representation of the various aspects of traditional Chinese good luck pictures. On top of this, research has been done on each picture, and the interpretations complement the visuals nicely.

As the five blessings are the aspiration of each individual, good luck delights all households. The good luck pictures originated in China and their good message should benefit all people of this world. May the *Designs of Chinese Blessings* bring good luck to your life and happiness to your family.

Huang Quanxin

Jan.1, 2003

一本万利

A small investment brings a ten-thousand -fold profit

《史记》："天下熙熙，皆为利来；天下攘攘，皆为利往。"旧时除夕夜迎财神和大年初二祭财神，都是春节期间的民俗活动。这种印有财神爷和吉利话的新春帖子，是供迎、祭祀财神用的，以求年初一分本，年底万分利之福。

"All the business and hustle of this world are aimed at money" – citation from the *Records of the Historian*. On the eve of the Chinese New Year and the second day of the New Year respectively, celebrations will be held and sacrifices made to the God of Money in folk customs. New Year cards with the portrait of fortune gods and words of good luck shown here are designed for these very occasions. They are expressions of hope for a small investment at the start of the year in exchange of a lot of returns at the end.

一多十余

In abundance and good fortune

《毛诗义疏》："鹭，水鸟。好白而洁，故谓之白鸟。"鹭为吉祥鸟。图为"一鹭食鱼"，古时"鹭"谐音为"多"，"食"谐"十"，"鱼"谐"余"，合为"一多十余"。表示财富多而有余，大吉大利。此图多见于古代传统吉祥印章之上。

Egret as a member of the bird species has been mentioned in very ancient Chinese records. It is considered a bird of good luck. The picture here depicts an egret eating fish and since "egret" shared the same pronunciation as "much" in the past, and "fish" as "plentiful", the message here is actually "in abundance and good fortune". The image often appears on ancient seals of good luck.

一掷百万

Immense returns with a small investment

《少年行》："一掷千金浑是胆，家徒四壁不知贫。"《晋书》："刘毅家无儋石之储，摴蒱一掷百万。"原指赌搏时一注就投下千金，后泛用以形容任意挥霍。而在吉祥图中却是指掷一金，而回报百万，以游戏形式恭喜发财。

Originally it meant to make a stake of a huge sum of money in gambling. It evolved to mean spending money unwisely and at random generally. In designs of happiness and good luck though, it means to get immense returns with a small investment. It is simply a way of greetings for fortune making in the form of games.

一掷千金

To put down a large sum of money

图中文：“宛转随阿堵，儿童不惮劳。千金凭一掷，意气和雄豪。”“阿堵”指钱。《世说新语》：“王夷甫雅尚玄远，常嫉其妇贪浊，口未尝言钱字。妇欲试之，令婢以钱绕床不得行。夷甫晨起，见钱阂行，呼婢曰：“举却阿堵物。”

The copy in the picture goes: “Even children fear not the trouble of the pursuit of *adu*; how heroic to put down a large sum of money”. “*Adu*” refers to money. It is recorded that a man devoted to elegant and lofty ideals detested his wife as avaricious and foul and would himself never utter the word “money”. His wife tested him and asked the maid to pile money round his bed so that he could not avoid it. Upon waking up the next morning, the man ordered the maid to remove “*adu*” so that he could move.

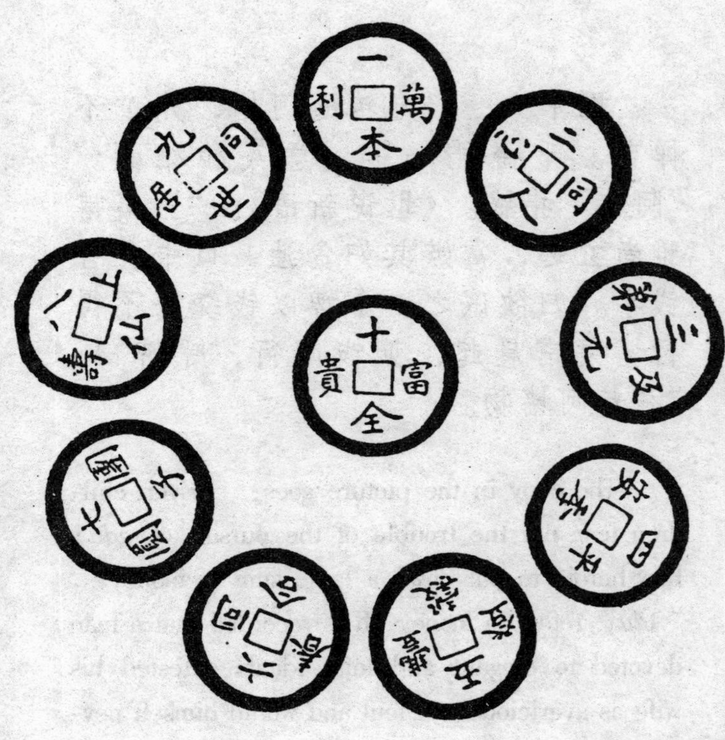

十全图

The picture of 10 coins

钱在古代又称泉，“泉”谐音“全”，十钱即十全，以十枚钱来寓意“十全十美”这一美好的颂词。十钱各有名目：一本万利，二人同心，三元及第，四季平安，五谷丰登，六合同春，七子团圆，八仙上寿，九世同居，十全富贵。

Money is also called “quan” in ancient China and “quan” shares the same pronunciation with “completeness”. So 10 coins of money implies “complete perfection”, an eulogy of good wishes. And the 10 coins have their own relevant description: a small investment in return of a lot of payback, two united as one under the same goal, entry in the top three in the royal examinations, peace and tranquility at all four seasons, a good harvest of all five kinds of grains, harmony in the six corners of the universe, reunion of the seven children in the family, birthday congratulations by the eight immortals, cohabitation of nine generations of people, and riches and honor in the complete.

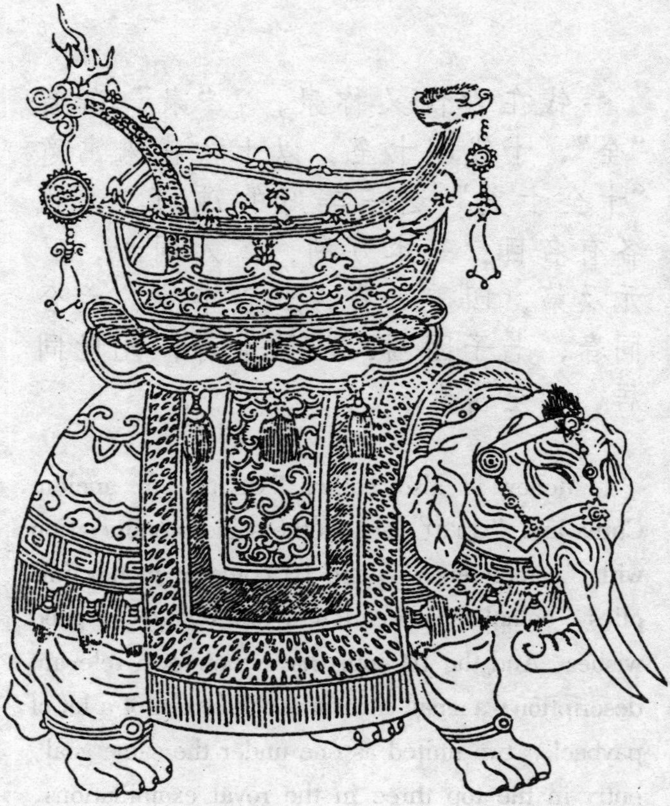

九贡

Nine kinds of tributes

《周礼·天官·大宰》：“以九贡致邦国之用：一曰祀贡；二曰嫔贡；三曰器贡；四曰币贡；五曰材贡；六曰货贡；七曰服贡；八曰斿贡；九曰物贡。”九贡，是周朝征收的九类贡物。大象带来九贡，寓财丰物博，大吉大祥。

The Rites of Zhou gives an account of the nine kinds of tributes offered to the emperor including sacrifices to Heaven and the gods, women as concubines to the emperor, utensils, money, clothes, etc. The image here depicts an elephant carrying these tributes, a sign of great volume of property and abundance of produce – surely extremely lucky and fortunate.

三猴烫猪

Three monkeys and a pig

图为民国初四川绵竹的条屏，三只头戴瓜皮帽的瘦猴与头戴礼帽的肥猪作纸牌赌博。三只猴子合谋作弊，也敌不过财多势大的黑猪。“猪”与“赌”音近、形似，猪贪得无厌，赌害人不浅。针对赌风日长的时弊，告诫时人勿贪赌废时。

This is a rectangular screen from Mianzhu, Sichuan Province, during the early period of the Republic of China. Three skinny monkeys in skullcaps are gambling against a fat pig in a hat. In vain did the monkeys conspire to cheat the powerful and rich pig. The Chinese characters for pig and gambling are similar both in sound and in form. As the pig is gluttonous in nature, gambling is doomed to bring along disasters. The picture serves to admonish those who indulge in gambling and waste their lives.

大吉图

The picture of great fortune

《风俗通义》："俗说鸡鸣将旦，为人起居，门亦昏闭晨开，捍难守固，礼贵报功。故门户用鸡。""鸡"与"吉"谐音，表示"大吉"。图中两只雄鸡各背负一盆摇钱树，树上有无数的金钱，表示"发财"，"大吉"必然"大发"。

Roosters crow to announce the arrival of the morning. Roosters serve to guard the door and announce news and this may be why they are kept at the doors. The word "rooster" sounds the same as "fortunate". In the picture, two roosters carry two trees with numerous coins on them and the coins fall when the trees are shaken, indicating good fortune. Wealth accumulates where fortune visits.

大吉大利

Extremely fortunate and smooth

古代最常见的钱是圆形方孔的铜钱，其形状取“天圆地方”，“外法天、内法地”之意。秦始皇时将其它各种形状的货币统一为这种形制，其后一直延用了两千余年。钱是财富的代表，图上还有金元宝及大吉大利字样，更是吉祥。

The most popular form of currency in ancient China is round-shaped copper coin with a square hole in the center. The design is associated with the concept of a round universe and square earth and following the universe externally and the earth internally. During the reign of the first emperor of the Qin Dynasty, this form was adopted to standardize Chinese currencies and the practice continued for over 2000 years. Money is the representative of wealth and rank and the shoe-shaped gold ingots and wordings of “extremely fortunate and smooth” further convey the message of fortune and good luck.

大吉大利

Extremely fortunate and prosperous

“桔”与“吉”谐，以大桔喻大吉，故桔为吉祥嘉瑞。《春秋运斗枢》：“旋星散为桔。”赋桔以神性。屈原曾作《桔颂》，以寓自己质朴坚贞。古人以栗木做神主。《太平御览》：“东门之栗，有靖家室。栗，木名，靖善也。”以大栗喻“大利”。

“Orange” sounds similar to “fortunate”, large oranges mean greatly fortunate, so oranges are signs of good luck. Oranges were seen as divine plants as ancient writings claimed oranges came from scattered rotating stars. Qu Yuan compared his modesty and loyalty to oranges in his *Ode to Oranges*. Chestnut trees were regarded divine in ancient times and believed to protect the whole family. Large chestnut trees imply “great prosperity”.

丰财聚宝

Getting rich and wealthy

崇拜财神，以求丰财聚宝。旧俗中的财神很多，图中为赵公明。《三教源流搜神大全》：头戴侧缨盔，身穿乌油甲，乌面黑髯，手持竹节钢鞭，跨下猛虎。手下有招宝、纳珍、招财、利市四名部下，都是专司金银财宝的神仙。

Worshipping the gods of fortune originated from the desire to get rich and wealthy. In ancient Chinese customs, there were lots of such gods and Zhao Gongming in the picture was just one of them. He was described as wearing a helmet with ribbons on the side, a glossy dark vest, black in the face with a dark beard, and riding on a fierce tiger with a whip in his hand. He had four subordinates under him – Zhao Bao (attracting treasure), Na Zhen (receiving jewelry), Jin Cai (introducing wealth), and Li Shi (profit), all immortals charging over gold, silver, and other treasures.

元宝成山

Piles of shoe-shaped gold ingots

元宝是中国古钱币的一种名称，后多指元朝以后铸成的马蹄形金银锭。银元宝亦称“宝银”、“马蹄银”，作货币流通。金元宝一般供保藏，极少流通。在旧俗中，元宝是财富的象征。“财”为“五福”之一，家有元宝成山，世代不愁吃穿。

Yuan Bao is a name for ancient Chinese currencies. It usually referred to shoe-shaped gold or silver ingots forged after the Yuan Dynasty. Silver ingots, also called “silver treasure” and “silver horse-hoof”, circulated as a form of currency while gold ingots were mostly used for collection. With *Yuan Bao* being a symbol of wealth, a family with piles and hills of these surely have no worries for generations to come.

元宝成山

Piles of shoe-shaped gold ingots

此图与上图为一对门童，旧时春节贴于院内门上，即有“多子”之吉，又有“多财”之祥。童子双手捧一大元宝，身旁还有成堆的元宝，以示“元宝成山”。元宝山上的火珠，是能聚光引火的珠，象征祥光普照，永不熄灭。

This picture and the one above form a pair of door boy designs pasted on doors inside the courtyard on the occasion of Chinese New Year in line with the lucky notion of “many children” and “a lot of wealth ”. The boy holds a large shoe-shaped gold ingot and next to him is a pile of gold ingots for the implication of hills of gold ingots. The flaming ball on top of the ingot hill serves to attract light and fire, implying that auspicious light shines over and will never extinguish.

五谷丰登

A bumper harvest of the five cereals

五谷丰登，是对太平盛世、丰收年景的祝颂。五谷为五种谷物：稻、黍、稷、麦、菽。《周礼·天官·疾医》：“以五味、五谷、五味养其病。”佛教密宗修法也使用五谷，以五谷泛指农作物。《汉书·郦食其传》：“民以食为天。”

A bumper harvest is an eulogy for a peaceful society in a rewarding year. The five cereals are rice, two kinds of millet, wheat and beans. *The Rites of Zhou* records that the five cereals serve to nourish people and cure them of diseases. The same five cereals are also used in Buddhism in spiritual cultivation. The five cereals refer to grains in general. The *Book of Han* states that food is of paramount importance.

五谷六畜

Five cereals and six livestock

五谷丰登，六畜兴旺，是农家最大的喜事。五谷指五种谷物，古代有多种说法。《素问·藏气法时论》："五谷为养。"六畜指马、牛、羊、猪、狗、鸡六种家畜（禽）。《左传》："古者六畜不相为用。"猪为中国农家的主要家畜。

Nothing delights the farmers more than a bumper harvest and well-multiplied livestock. While five cereals refer to five kinds of grains, the six farm animals are horse, ox, sheep, pig, dog and chicken. In the past, these six farm animals were raised for different purposes. Pigs are the main livestock Chinese farmers keep.

日进斗金

Earning large quantities of gold each day

旧时，各地“日进斗金”的门童年画，真是各俱特色。图中一穿着富贵的可爱童子，双手推一独轮车，车上装满大金元宝和大个火珠。火珠又称宝珠，是古神话中一种神奇的通灵宝物，是祥光普照、永照的吉祥，是龙戏之珠。

Ancient New Year pictures featuring “earning large quantities of gold each day” took on different forms and designs. In the picture is a lovely boy fabulously dressed pushing a one-wheeled cart with large gold ingots and a large flaming ball inside. The flaming ball is also called the treasure pearl, a magic object that could communicate with the spirits in ancient fables. It shines forever to bring good luck and fortune. The ball is the plaything of the dragons.

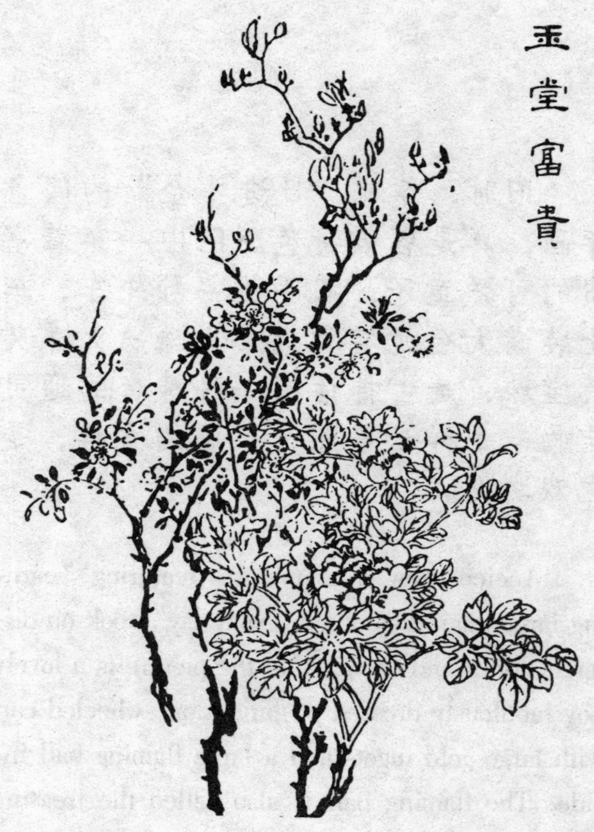

玉堂富贵

Wealth and rank in harmonious and well-off families

《三辅黄图·汉宫》:“建章宫南有玉堂……阶陛皆玉为之。”玉堂指汉代宫殿。《游天台山赋》:“朱阙玲珑于林间，玉堂阴映于高隅。”又指神仙所居之处。也泛指富贵、和睦之家。玉兰取其“玉”，海棠谐其“堂”，牡丹花取其“富贵”。

In ancient Chinese historical records, “jade houses” refer to the palaces of the Han Dynasty or the dwelling places of the fairies. The phrase evolved to mean harmonious and well-off families generally. In the picture, *yulan* magnolia has the sound of “jade” and Chinese flowering crabapples carry the sound of “house”. Peony flowers imply “wealth and rank”.

玉堂富贵

Wealth and rank in harmonious and well-off families

玉堂原指宫殿、仙居等，后泛指吉祥之家。牡丹乃花中之王，又称富贵花。玉堂富贵用于赞颂家庭和睦、富贵有余。此图以“鱼塘”谐音“玉堂”，背景为牡丹花表示“富贵”，合为“玉堂富贵”。旧时，这种童子抱骑金鱼形式的吉祥图很多。

“Jade house” originally refers to palaces and homes of the celestial beings; it gradually became a common term for families enjoying harmony and good fortune. Peony flowers, the queen of flowers, are also known as flowers of wealth and rank. The phrase is an eulogy to harmonious families that enjoy a good livelihood. In the picture, “fish pond” shares the same sound with “jade house”, the peony flowers at the background stand for wealth and rank. In old times, the design of a child riding on a fish was a popular form of pictures featuring good luck.

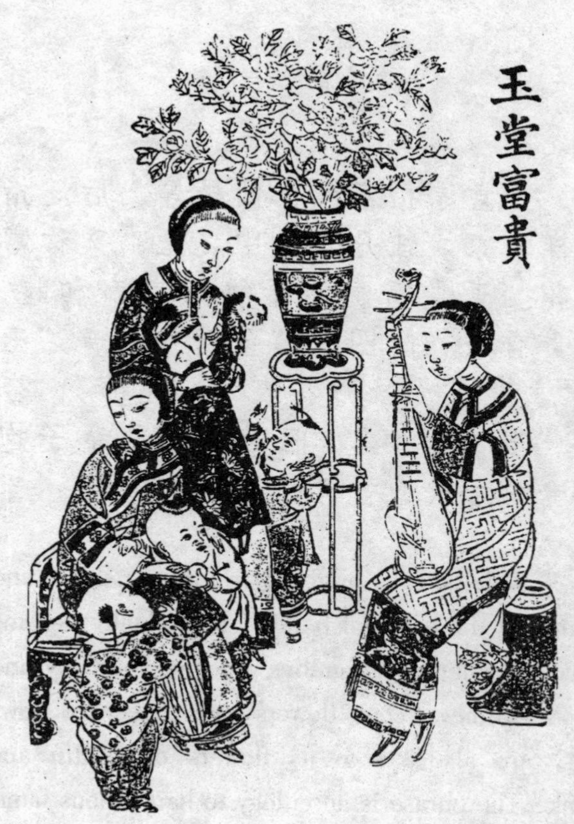

玉堂富贵

Wealth and rank in harmonious and well-off families

此图，为清代苏州的年画。玉堂即是汉代殿名，又是嫔妃所居之处。《汉书》："抑损椒房玉堂之盛宠，毋听后宫之请谒。"注："玉堂嬖幸之舍也。"民间以玉堂示家庭，图中母子在听苏州特有的弹词，堂上牡丹示"富贵"。

This is a New Year picture of Suzhou from the Qing Dynasty. Jade house is the name for Han palaces and the place where the concubines stayed (the reference for this may be found in the *Book of Han*). In folk customs, jade house refers to families. In our picture here, a mother and her son are listening to a special kind of musical lyrics of Suzhou. The peony in the hall implies wealth and rank.

功名富贵

Official rank leads to wealth

大鸡作为“大吉”之物，备“五德”。鸡鸣将旦，光明到来，以“公鸣”谐音“功名”。刘禹锡《同乐天送令狐相公赴东都留守》：“世上功名兼将相，人间声价是文章。”苏轼《墨宝堂论》：“士当以功名闻于世。”功成名就自有富贵。

A large rooster sounds the same as “extremely fortunate”. The crowing of the rooster announces the arrival of the morning and light. “Rooster crowing” sounds the same as “official rank”. In poems by Liu Yuxi of the Tang Dynasty and Su Shi of the Song Dynasty, the importance of seeking high official ranks was given much significance as it was part of the heroic pursuit of the time. High official ranks naturally lead to wealth in life.

功名富贵

Official rank leads to wealth

功名富贵，即功成名遂、富贵荣华。《墨子》："功成名遂，名誉不可虚假。"《史记》："昔者中山之国，地方五百里，赵独吞之，功成名立而利附焉。"《潜夫论》："所谓贤人君子者，非必高位厚禄富贵荣华之谓也。"

"Official rank leads to wealth" refers to the situation where one is accomplished in achievements and fame and enjoys the riches and prestige brought along. In ancient Chinese historical records such as *Records of the Historian*, seeking achievements and fame is advocated. Moreover, it is emphasized that all virtuous people are inevitably people in high posts of fame and riches.

功名富贵

Official rank leads to wealth

宋·欧阳修《相州昼锦堂记》："仕宦而至将相，富贵而归故乡。此人情之所荣，而今昔之所同也。"雄鸡司晨，守夜有时，故古代帝王"以鸡为候"。图以公鸡鸣叫之"公鸣"谐音"功名"。而以牡丹示富贵，合为"功名富贵"。

Ouyang Xiu of the Song Dynasty said this in one of his poems: "Seek high official posts and return to one's hometown in wealth. This is what everyone considers honorable and the practice since ancient times". As the rooster watches over the hours and announces the arrival of morning, ancient emperors and kings regarded roosters highly. In the picture, "rooster crowing" sounds the same as "official rank" and peony flowers indicate wealth and rank. So the visuals combine to imply "official rank leads to wealth".

平安富贵

Peace and wealth

瓶的造型很多，葫芦瓶因形似葫芦而得名，多用于陈设。葫芦与“福禄”谐音。“瓶”谐音“平”以寓平安。宋朝周敦颐《爱莲说》：“牡丹，花之富贵者也。”牡丹的“富贵花”之名大约始于此时。合为：平平安安，富贵有余。

Bottles take after many designs and gourd bottles, shaped like bottle gourds, are often used for display. Gourd shares the same sound as "happiness and good fortune". Bottle sounds the same as "peace". In *An Ode to Lotus*, Zhou Dunyi of the Song Dynasty called peonies the flowers of wealth and rank, which may very well be the beginning of such association. The picture here sends this message: peace and wealth.

平安富贵

Peace and wealth

《汉书·陈遵传》："观瓶之居，居井之眉。"瓶，最早为汲水器或容器，后多作摆设，如花瓶等。瓶中安放牡丹花，以"瓶"、"安"谐音"平安"，以富贵花示"富贵"，寓意平平安安、富贵如意。还有以竹报平安、富贵花开，合为"平安富贵"。

Bottles when first made were for fetching water or use as utensils. Later, bottles began to be used as objects of display such as holding flowers. Peony flowers in bottles has this connotation: peaceful and wealthy to the heart's content with "bottle" meaning peace and peony flowers standing for wealth and rank. Pictures of the same theme may have bamboo and peony flowers on them.

龙抬头

The dragon raises its head

《宛署杂记·民风》："都人呼二月二为龙抬头，乡民用灰自门外蜿蜒，布入宅厨，施绕水缸呼为引龙回。"中和节后，草木萌生，百虫复活。引龙回，请龙兴云播雨，以求农业丰收；龙为百虫之精，驱五毒，以求人健居安。

Records of folk practice describe how country folks would draw a line with ashes from outside the yard to the kitchen and around the water jar to call the dragon back on February 2nd. In early spring, plants and grasses come back to life and animals wake up from a long sleep. The dragon is called back to arrange for clouds and rains so that there will be a harvest of crops. As the dragon is the head of all animals, it has the function of driving away harmful insects and safeguarding man and their dwelling places.

出门见喜

To see magpies on stepping out of home

传说乾隆在前门楼上问刘墉，楼下街市上有多少人，刘墉不知。乾隆说只有两个人，一个是“名”，一个是“利”，人来人往无非追名逐利。时值春暖花开，丈夫要外出挣钱，妻儿一直送到门外，正见喜鹊，寓“出门见喜大发财”。

According to anecdote, once on the tower of Qianmen in Beijing, the emperor Qianlong asked his minister Liu Yong how many people there were on the streets below and Liu Yong answered he did not know. The emperor said there were only two, namely fame and profit and all the business and hustle out there was for but the pursuit of fame and profit. The picture here stages spring time. The husband is about to leave his hometown to earn money. As his wife and child see him off, they see a magpie right outside their house. The implication is the sight of happiness (the name of the bird) promises good fortune.

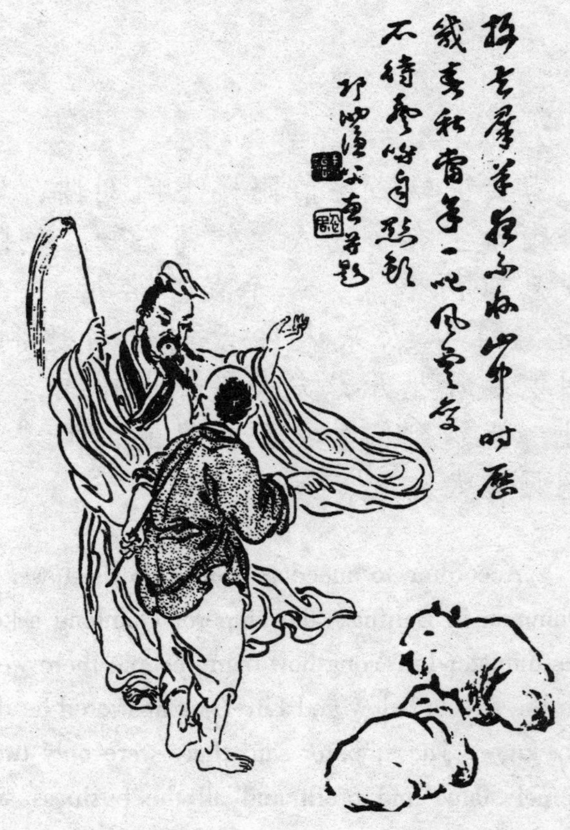

叱石为羊

A shout at the stones turn them back into sheep

《金华府志》:"晋,黄初平,兰溪人。牧羊遇道士,将至金华石室中。兄初起寻之四十余年,一日逢道士,引入山相见。问羊安在?初平曰:'在山之东。'初起视之,但见白石。初平叱之,石皆成羊。"黄初平为道教仙人。

The local records of Jinhua have this story: Huang Chuping of the Jin Dynasty was tending sheep when he came across a Taoist priest who took him to a stone room where he never left ever since. His brother Chuqi looked for him for round 40 years. Finally Chuqi was led to the stone room by a priest. Upon his brother's request after the sheep, Chuping answered they were at the east of the mountain. But Chuqi saw nothing but white stones. At this, Chuping shouted at the stones and they turned back to sheep. Huang Chuping was an immortal of the Taoist school.

瓜瓞富贵

Generations of children, wealth and good fortune

“绵绵瓜瓞”出自《诗经》，瓞，小瓜。是说周朝的祖先像瓜瓞一样岁岁相继，一直传到太王才奠定了王业基础。后转用于子孙昌盛，图中以“瓜”示“瓜”，以“蝶”谐“瓞”，合为“瓜瓞”。富贵童子持蝶踏瓜，寓子孙满堂、富贵吉祥。

Melons of large and small sizes growing on long vines is a sign of lasting generations of offsprings. The phrase comes from the *Book of Songs*, which gives an account of the long and succeeding generations of the ancestors of the Zhou Dynasty whose foundation was finally formed at the reign of Emperor Wen of Zhou. The phrase evolved to refer to lots of children and grandchildren. The picture here features a child in luxurious clothing holding a butterfly and stepping on melons. The message is one of many children, great fortune and harmonious life.

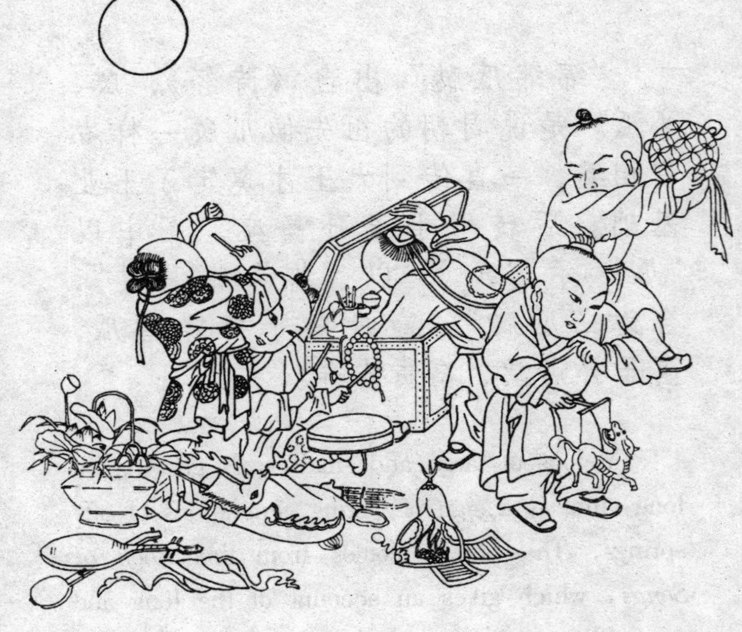

生意兴隆

Prosperous business

“生意兴隆通四海，财源茂盛达三江。”旧时的买卖、店铺多有此类恭颂发财的楹联，还如：“经之营之财恒足矣，悠也久也利莫大焉。”在旧时春节，贴有“货郎图”，一方面表示货郎生意兴隆，另一方面货郎给带来过节用品。

“A thriving business extends to the far reaches of the four seas and its abundance of transactions cover the whole nation”. Couplets of this kind are often hung on the pillars of shops as a form of good wishes for making money. Similar couplets include: “There is always plenty of goods to sell and the profits extend a long period of time”. The picture of the traveling peddler was a common New Year picture in old times. On the one hand, it indicated the peddler had good business, on the other, the peddler brought along goods and articles needed for the festival.

生肖发财

To make a fortune every year

我国古代术数家用十二种动物来配十二地支，子为鼠，丑为牛，寅为虎，卯为兔，辰为龙，巳为蛇，午为马，未为羊，申为猴，酉为鸡，戌为狗，亥为猪。后以为人生在某年就肖某物，称为“十二生肖”，生肖发财意为年年发财。

Ancient Chinese astrologists matched the 12 Earthly Branches (signs of order) with 12 animals: the first is the rat, the second the ox, the third the tiger, the fourth the hare, the fifth the dragon, the sixth the snake, the seventh the horse, the eighth the sheep, the ninth the monkey, the tenth the rooster, the 11th the dog, and the 12th the boar. Later, a person born in a particular year came to be associated with the animal of that particular year and the 12 animals became symbolic animals.

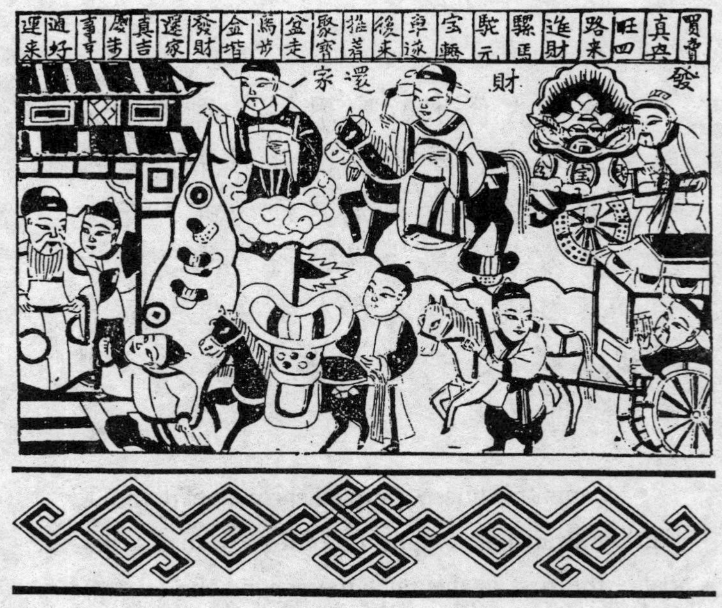

发财还家

Return home after making a lot of money

发财还家是做买卖人的吉祥，图文："买卖真兴旺，四路来进财，骡马驮元宝，轿车随后来，推着聚宝盆，走马步金階。发财还家真吉庆，万事亨通好运来。"旧时年画中，发财还家的内容很多，上面还有许多押韵的吉利话，盼望发财。

To return home after making a lot of money is the good luck all business people desire for. The poem in the picture reads like this: "A flourishing business brings in profits from all transactions in all places. Gold and silver ingots on donkeys and horses, and a sedan-chair follows behind. What a happy event to be homeward bound after making money, and how fortunate to have a smooth path for all things that come along the way". There are lots of other New Year pictures of this theme with similarly lucky words in rhymes to wish for wealth.

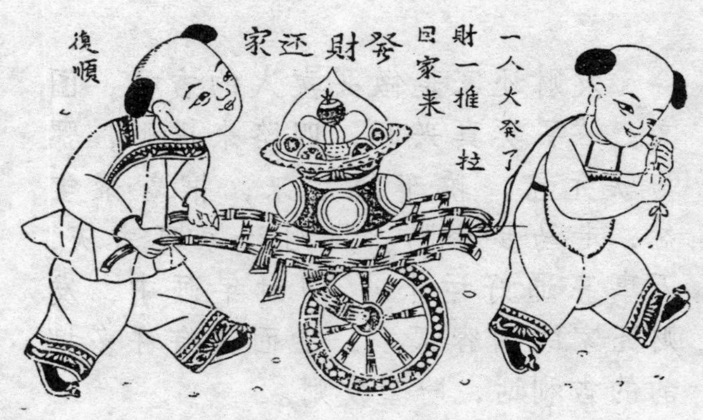

发财还家

Return home after making a lot of money

"一人大发了财，一推一拉回家来"。图中两位童子，一位童子在前拉车，一位童子在后推独轮车。车上有一聚宝盆，盆中金钱、元宝、宝珠等各种财宝。家庭生活的各种开销，都要落实到"钱"上，故盼望"发财还家"。

"As business has been profitable, two are needed to pull and push the treasure home". There are two boys in the picture, one is pulling the cart at the front, the other is pushing it at the back. On the cart is a treasure bowl with money, shoe-shaped gold and silver ingots, and jade and treasure, etc. All expenditure needed to run a household must be supported by money. This is why the family expects their family members to return home with their proceeds from business.

发财还家

Return home after making a lot of money

“一人大发了财，两人一抬回家来”。图中两位童子，前面一位童子手执如意，后面一位童子怀抱金钱。二人抬一聚宝盆，盆中有金银财宝，高高兴兴地发财回家。《申鉴·政体》：“天下之本在家。”家中财源不断是福。

“As business has been profitable, two are needed to carry the treasure home” . There are two boys in the picture, the one at the front holds a *ruyi* and the one behind holds money. Carrying a treasure bowl full of gold, silver, and other treasures, the two are happily heading home. As ancient Chinese stress the importance of families, continuous inflow of wealth into the house is surely a blessing.

吉庆有余

Good fortune and plentiful sustenance

磬，中国古代宫廷打击乐器，周朝时就设有磬师。中国古磬大体有两种，悬一面独奏者为“持磬”，悬多面合奏者为“编磬”。磬用石或玉或金属制成，其音清亮悦耳，常以“声如磬”形容上好的瓷器。以“吉磬”配“有鱼”，寓吉庆有余。

Chime stone is a royal percussion musical instrument of ancient China. Masters playing the chime stones existed as early as the Zhou Dynasty. It was made of stone, jade or metal. Because of the clear and pleasant sound it makes, comparison has often been made between chime stone and porcelain of good quality on account of the sound. The chime stone (celebration) and the fish (plentiful) together imply happiness and surplus.

吉庆有余

Good fortune and plentiful sustenance

磬为“五瑞”之一，也为“八宝”之一，是吉祥之物。图中一童子用手击磬，寓意“吉庆”。另一童子伴磬乐喜舞鱼灯，以寓意“有余”，合为“吉庆有余”。新春伊始，两位童子在家中庭院击乐磬，舞鱼灯，以颂“吉庆有余”之吉祥。

Chime stone as one of the five auspicious objects and of the eight treasures is an article of good fortune. One boy beating at the chime stone in the picture stands for happiness and celebration. The other boy dancing with a fish lantern to the music implies surplus. At the beginning of a new spring, two boys are playing with a musical instrument and dancing in their courtyard, a picture celebrating the blessing of good fortune and abundance of life.

吉庆有余

Good fortune and plentiful sustenance

图中以“戟”谐音“吉”，以“磬”谐音“庆”，又以云纹磬上挂有鱼，示“有余”，合为“吉庆有余”。此吉祥图又含“平升三级”之吉庆。以“瓶”谐音“平”，以瓶纹“旭日东升”示“升”，以“三戟”谐音“三级”。

The halberd in the picture sounds the same as “good luck”, chime stone implies “celebration”, the fish on the chime stone with clouds stands for “surplus”, jointly good fortune and plentiful sustenance. This picture of good luck has another meaning – the bottle and the rising sun stands for promotion while the three halberds imply three levels. So the celebration is for a large promotion as well.

吉庆有余

Good fortune and plentiful sustenance

童子右手执“戟”示“吉”，左手提“磬”示“庆”。磬上之鱼示“有余”。《诗经》：“修我矛戟，与子偕作。”戟为古代兵器，后戟也成为官阶、武勋的象征。唐代，官、阶、勋达三品之家，可立戟于门，称为“戟门”或“戟户”。

The boy holding a halberd in the right hand and a chime stone in the left hand with a fish on it forms a picture of good luck, celebration, and surplus. The halberd is an ancient weapon, and later evolved to symbolize official title and military achievements. In the Tang Dynasty, households with the third rank of title or above are allowed to post a halberd to their gate.

双鱼吉庆

Good fortune and abundance

“晋砖五鹿宜子孙，汉洗双鱼大吉羊”。“双鱼吉庆”的吉祥图纹在汉代已有。汉代铜洗底部绘对鱼，侧面题有“大吉羊”三字。“双鱼吉庆”图案多在结婚用品上用，以祝夫妻吉庆。

“Five deer on a brick of the Jin Dynasty bless the children and double fish on a basin of the Han Dynasty send wishes of happiness and joy”. The lucky design of “double fish happiness” was first seen during the Han Dynasty. A basin from the Han Dynasty was found to have double fish on its bottom and characters indicating great fortune on the side. The picture is often seen on articles for marriage as a way of celebrating and blessing the newly-weds.

厌胜钱

Yansheng coin

厌胜钱是铸成钱币形式的吉利品或避邪品。《博古图》:“厌胜钱有五,一体之间,龙马并著,形长而方。李孝美号之曰厌胜钱。”自汉以来即有铸造,上面有各种吉祥语和吉祥图。厌胜钱不是货币,仅供佩戴玩赏。

Yansheng coin, forged in the shape of money, is an article for good luck or for warning off evil. *Yansheng* coin was first forged during the Han Dynasty. There are five kinds of such coin. In long and square shapes, it has designs of a horse and dragon on it as well as words and visuals of good luck. *Yansheng* coin is no currency and can only be used as accessories and for appreciation.

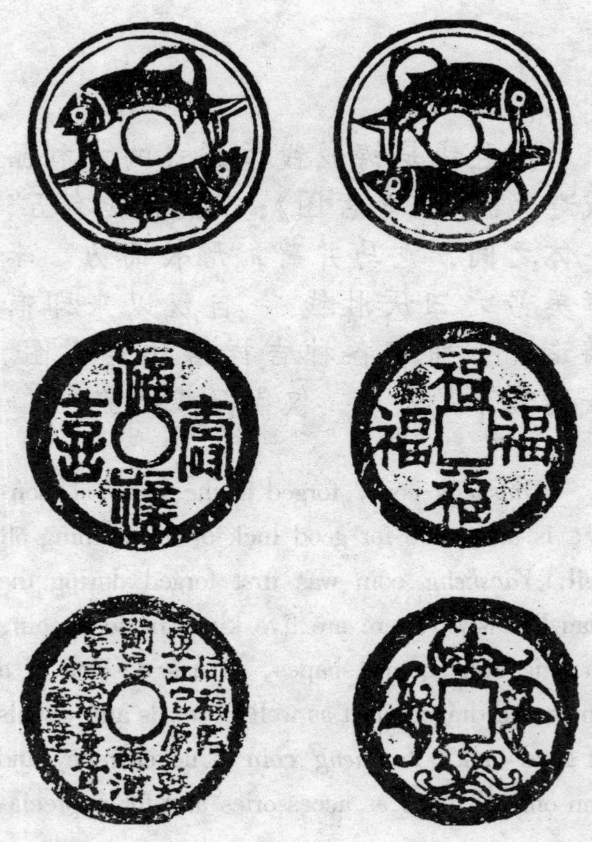

压胜钱

Yasheng coin

厌胜钱亦称压胜钱。厌胜是古代的一种巫术，谓能诅咒制服人或物。而厌胜钱则是铸成钱币形式的避邪品或吉利品。此图中有双鱼钱，福禄寿喜钱，背面有五言绝句吉祥诗一首。四福钱，背面三只蝙蝠飞翔，表示“福在眼前”。

Yansheng coin is also called *Yasheng* coin. It is used to warn off evil or to wish for good luck. In this picture, there are designs of double fish and blessing-fortune-longevity and a poem of good luck at the back. There are also designs of three flying bats, indicating "happiness is just here".

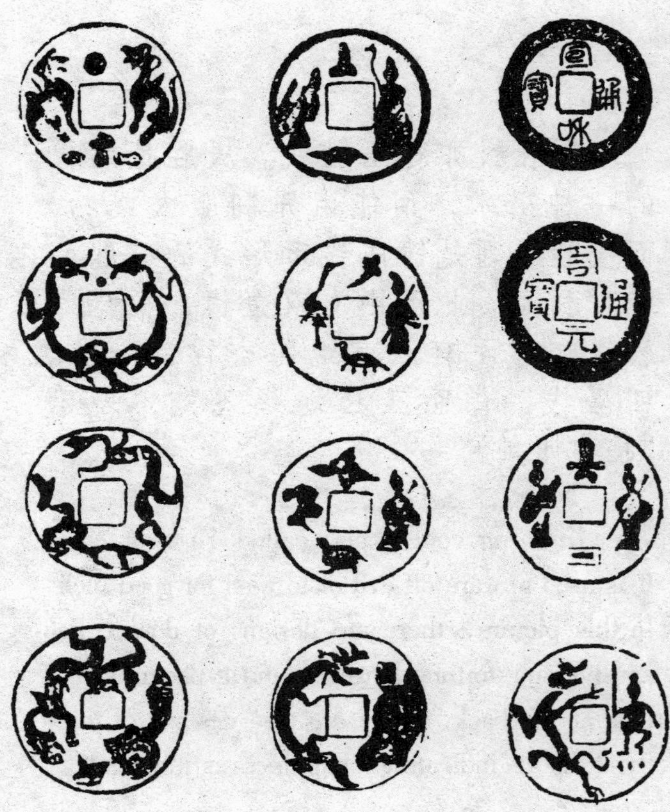

压 岁 钱

End-of-the-year money

压岁钱是旧时春节长辈给小孩的钱。《燕京岁时记·压岁钱》："以彩绳穿钱，编作龙形，置于床脚，谓之压岁钱。尊长之赐小儿者，亦谓之压岁钱。"压岁钱最早是除夕夜给鬼怪的，以使不抓小孩，后来变成过节给小孩的钱。

End-of-the-year money is given to children by the elder members of the family during the New Year. Records about Beijing tell us that end-of-the-year money consisted of coins tied up with colorful threads into the shape of a dragon and placed at the feet of beds. Later, it referred to money given to children by their parents, or elders. At the start, end-of-the-year money was prepared for the evil spirits so that they wouldn't grab the children. It evolved to be money for children at the end of the year.

年年有余

Great abundance every year

俗话说："没有鱼不成席"，逢年过节自然少不了鱼，也少不了爆竹，图中已是一派过节的景象。提篮中的两条鲶鱼，即谐音"年年"又表示"有余"。"年年有余家家乐，岁岁平安户户欢"。"年年有余"吉联在旧时春节处处可见。

An idiom says that "a feast without fish is not a banquet". Fish and firecrackers are indispensable items for festivals and the New Year. The picture depicts the occasion of festive celebration. The two catfish in the basket sound the same as "year after year" and implies "great abundance" as well. "Every household is happy as they lead a peaceful and abundant life year after year". The picture is a common scene in New Year in old times.

年年有余

Great abundance every year

此图与下图为一对门童年画。旧时街门贴门神，屋门贴门童，以避邪、祈福。旧时这种身穿兜兜、怀抱鱼的童子形象，在年画中常有出现，如：富贵有余、玉堂富贵、金玉满堂、连年有余等。门童年画是旧时吉祥画的重要形式。

The picture and the one following this form a pair of New Year pictures. In old times, pictures of gate god were pasted on gates facing the street and pictures of boys on doors inside to beg for protection and blessing. The image of a boy in belly-band holding a fish is a common feature of New Year pictures in old times. New Year pictures of door boys are an important part of pictures of good luck in old times.

年年有余

Great abundance every year

每幅门童画上各有两个大字，四字合为“年年有余”，以示成双、对对。图中充满画面、占据主体的童子，怀抱两条鲶鱼，以示“年年有余”。图中的富贵花与鱼，又示“富贵有余”。图中卐字纹与桃，又示“万寿”，可谓一图多福。

There are two large characters on each door boy picture to represent the idea of being double and in pairs. Together, the two pictures form "great abundance every year". Taking up most of the space in the picture, the boy carries two catfish, indicating abundance every year. The peony flowers and fish in the picture also means abundance of wealth and the symbol 卐 and peach in the picture send the message of longevity. It is a picture of multiple blessings.

农家忙

Busy with farm work

“锄禾日当午，汗滴禾下土，谁知盘中餐，粒粒皆辛苦”。“春种一粒粟，秋收万颗子”。耕田种地是旧时人们最主要的生产活动。春天来了，人们开始忙于春耕。一分耕耘，一分收获，庄稼忙、农家乐是年画的重要题材。

“As the farmer ploughs the field at noon, drops of sweat fall on earth below. Grateful diners should bear in mind that each grain on their plate comes from hard labor”. “A grain of cereal planted in spring time brings harvest in autumn”. Field cultivation is a major form of production people were engaged in the past. The arrival of spring calls for the farmers to start another round of busy work. Labor brings rewards. To get busy with farm work is a major theme of New Year pictures.

农家乐

The joy of farmers

宋·李之仪《鹧鸪天》："从今认得归田乐，何必桃源是故乡。"民以食为天，农以耕为乐。图中一老农于种地之余在田头小息，这时儿孙们给老人送来茶水，老人高兴的一手扇扇驱暑，一手摇鼓逗孙，充满农家的欢乐。

Ancient Chinese scholars like Tao Yuanming regarded farm work a joy of life. As a nation relies on food to sustain and grow, farmers take delight in field farm work. In the picture is an old farmer at rest on the fields. As his grandchildren send him tea, the old man is joyfully blowing the fan with one hand and teasing his little grandson with a drum with another. The picture fully illustrates the joy of farming.

艾葉交香增五福

桃符書赤慶三多

天成

刘海戏蟾

Liu Hai teases the toad

《湖广总志》："刘元英号海蟾子，广陵人，仕燕王刘守光为相。有道人求谒，索鸡卵十枚，金钱十枚，置几上累卵于钱，若浮屠状，海蟾惊叹曰：'危哉!'道人曰：'人居欢乐之场，其危有甚于此者。'"海蟾大悟，易服从道。民间多有刘海戏蟾、戏钱图。

Liu Yuanying, also called Haichan (sea toad), was once a minister. A Taoist priest came to visit him one day and asked for ten eggs and ten coins of money. The priest placed the eggs on the coins to form a pagoda. And Haichan acclaimed it "dangerous". The priest then said that those in the midst of merriment are more dangerous than this. Haichan was totally enlightened. He changed clothes and converted to Taoism.

花开富贵

Blooming peony flowers greet fortune

“花开富贵”与前面的一幅“竹报平安”，为一对“门童”。意为：平安保佑積善之门，富贵常临忠厚之家。童子手捧盛开牡丹——富贵花的瓶，足登长有灵芝仙草的寿石，两旁又有金钱、元宝。春暖花开日，富贵降家时。

“Blooming peony flowers greet fortune” and “Bamboo announces peace and tranquility” form a pair of door boy pictures, meaning households stressing kindness are protected with peace and honest families tend to have wealth. The boy holds a bottle of peony flowers and stands on a longevity stone with glossy ganoderma with money and ingots of gold and silver beside. As flowers bloom in warm weather, fortune comes on the door steps.

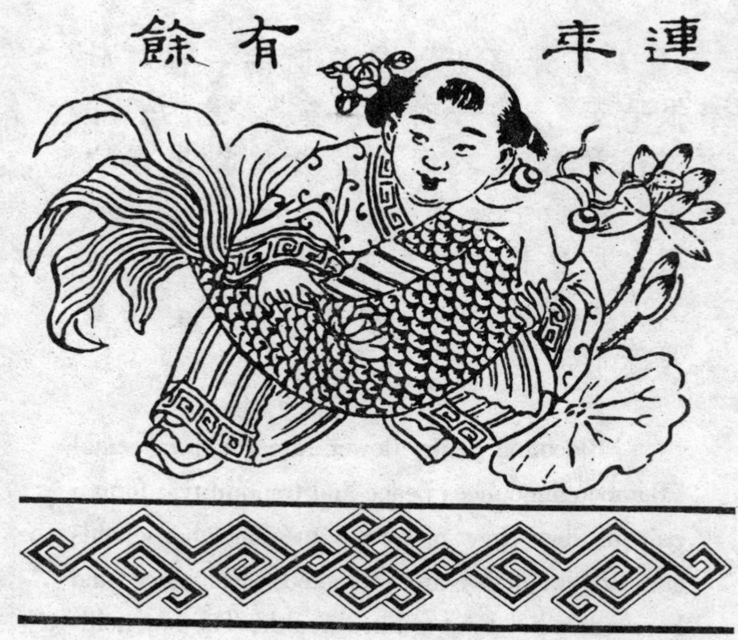

连年有余

Abundance year after year

《荀子·富国》：“下富则上富。”《国策·秦策五》：“今力田疾作，不得暖衣余食。”高诱注：“余，饶。”《说文解字》：“饶，饱也。”《吕氏春秋·辨土》：“无使不足，亦无使有余。”余者多余。图以“莲”、“鱼”谐音喻“连年有余”。

Ancient Chinese philosophers stress the importance of a rich and affluent nation and people and the balance between abundance and scarcity. The fish and the lotus flowers in the picture mean abundance year after year.

连年有余

Abundance year after year

《礼记·王制》："国无九年之蓄曰'不足'，无六年之蓄曰'急'，无三年之蓄曰'国非其国'也。"韩愈在《太原王公墓志铭》中云："在官四年，数其积蓄，钱余于库，米余于廪。"不想有"国非之国"之灾，须有"连年有余"之福。

Ancient Chinese stressed such principles of state governing: inadequacy occurs where a nation does not have enough savings to sustain it for nine years; where a nation lacks savings for six years, it is tight; if a nation does not even have enough to sustain its people for three years, it is no longer a nation. Han Yu of the Tang Dynasty had such self-comment: during the four years at post, I had made savings for the office both in money and in grains. To avoid the disaster of failing to be a nation, there must be abundance year on year.

连年有余

Abundance year after year

在中国数千年的封建社会中，是“遍身罗绮者，不是养蚕人。十指不沾泥，鳞鳞居大厦。”广大劳动人民却是“陶尽门前土，屋上无片瓦。”整天为生活着急，不敢奢望年年有余，只求天天有粮，不再朝不保夕。故“连年有余”图备受欢迎。

In the thousands of years of feudal ruling in China, those clad in silk did not raise silkworms and those resided in large buildings did not build a brick. The massive working class labored all their life and still lived with no roof above their head. As they toiled for life, they dared not hope for abundance year after year. Their desire was simply to have enough food for each day. This is why pictures featuring abundance year after year get so popular.

连年有余

Abundance year after year

在中国，鱼为吉祥之物。古代有“鱼符”，又称“鱼契”，为权力信物。据载唐朝时曾赐发给百官以“鱼符”，木雕或铜铸成鱼形，上面刻字，合半为一，以为凭物。“鱼”与“余”谐音，故以“鱼”示“余”。余者富之余，连年有富余。

Fish is an object of good luck in China. There were fish tallies or deeds in ancient China as tokens of power. In the Tang Dynasty, the officials were issued fish tallies of wood or copper with carvings as tokens. As fish shares the sound of “abundance”, it is often quoted to convey that meaning. A fortunate thing it is to have material and money to spare at the end of the year and abundance year after year is the wish of all people.

连年有余

Abundance year after year

"有余"是人们对幸福生活的渴望，故"有余"的吉祥图颇多。如：吉庆有余、富贵有余、年年有余等。图中多以"莲"谐音"连"，表示"连年"。"弥陀之净土，以莲花为所居。"莲既是佛国之物，又是"花中君子"、吉祥之花。

To have abundance in life is a common wish which explains why good luck pictures of this theme are so popular. There is great fortune and abundance year on year, wealth and abundance year after year, etc. Lotus flowers share the sound of "continuity" and here it indicates year after year. As an article from the realm of Buddhism, lotus flowers are gentlemen of flowers and messengers of auspicious signs.

连钱财丰

Strings of coins and abundance in wealth

古钱是由武器、农具等演变而来。《国语·周语下》："景王二十一年，将铸大钱。"这里的钱已指铜铸币。王莽时称钱为泉。《素问》："始于一，终于九焉。"九为极数示多，九枚钱币串在一起，以示货币充足，财富丰厚。

Ancient coins evolved from weapons and agricultural tools. Copper coins were first minted in the Zhou Dynasty. As nine is the number indicating extreme in quantity since ancient China, a string of nine coins is the message of sufficiency in currencies and abundance in wealth.

财神献宝

The gods of fortune bring treasure

旧时，除夕迎财神，初二祭财神。财神庙一年只初二开放，梵香膜拜，以祈赐财。祭品为活鲤鱼和鲜羊肉，以“鱼”、“羊”取“鲜”，以祈新（鲜）年再发新财。午餐要食“元宝汤”（馄饨），到街上买些纸元宝，示财神献宝。

In old times, New Year eve was the occasion to greet the gods of fortune and January 2nd the day to offer them sacrifices. Temples of fortune gods were opened only on the second of January when people came to burn incenses and bow to the gods to beg for wealth. To fulfil one's wish to be blessed to get rich the next year, sacrifices should be live carp and fresh mutton as the Chinese character "fresh" (sounding similar to new) is formed with the two characters "fish" and "mutton". For lunch, soup of gold and silver ingots (wantons) should be served, paper in the shape of gold ingots should be offered – meaning the gods of fortune will bring the worshipper treasure.

文武财神

Civil and military gods of fortune

民间供奉的财神，主要分文财神和武财神两种。财神越多，财源越多，所以在文武财神的吉祥图中，还多配有与财有关的仙人、童子等。以及单独成幅的“文财神”、“武财神”、“五路财神”、“青龙财神”、“增福财神”等。

Gods of fortune worshipped by the people were mostly two kinds: civil and military. The more fortune gods there are, the more resources of money. Therefore, in good luck pictures featuring civil and military gods of fortune, immortals and boys related to the gods are often seen as well. There are also separate pictures of civil god of fortune, military god of fortune, fortune gods of all directions, fortune god of the green dragon, and fortune god of extra blessings, etc.

文武财神献宝

Civil and military gods of fortune send over treasure

图中的文武财神，分别手捧元宝和火珠，以示“文武财神献宝”。文武财神身旁还有几位献宝、引钱的童子。图正中的大象身驮聚宝盆、摇钱树。聚宝盆、摇钱树是聚宝、生财之物，以示“财神献宝、财源不断。”大象则示吉祥。

The civil and military gods of fortune are holding gold ingots and a flaming ball in their hands in the picture. Beside them are the boys that serve to present treasure and introduce money. The elephant in the center of the picture carries a treasure bowl and a tree that sheds money when shaken. The message is “gods of fortune present treasure and money to their worshippers who now have endless wealth to come in”. The elephant is an animal of good luck.

财神接财神

The gods of fortune greet the gods of fortune

增福财神端坐在聚财厅的正中，其左右分别为文财神、武财神，还有招财童子、利市仙官，以及戏金蟾之刘海等财神。真是财神接财神，喜赴聚财厅，以示财神光临府第。财神面前供奉着元宝等，聚财厅旁还有两株摇钱树。

The fortune god of extra blessings is sitting upright in the center of the hall of gathered treasures. To his left and right are the civil god of fortune and the military god of fortune. Also present are the boys to attract wealth and the fairy that brings profits as well as Liu Hai the toad teaser. What a lively scene with so many gods of fortune gathered together. It actually indicates all the fortune gods have made their presence to the house of the worshipper. Gold and silver ingots are displayed in front of the gods. At the side of the treasure gathering hall are two trees that shed money when shaken.

武 财 神

The military god of fortune

武财神指赵公元帅，姓赵名朗，字公明。秦时避世修道，汉张道陵入鹤鸣山，收之为徒。张天师炼丹成功，赵公明食之成仙，被封为“正一玄坛赵元帅”。赵公明黑面浓须，顶盔披甲，坐骑黑虎，持宝撵鞭。《封神榜》中也有个赵公明。

This refers to general Zhao, who had two names: Lang and Gongming. At the time of the Qin Dynasty, he retreated to practice Taoism. Zhang Daoling of the Han Dynasty accepted him as a disciple, gave him a pill of immortality and a Taoist title of general. Zhao Gongming is dark-faced with a thick beard. He is in helmet and armor, rides a black tiger, and holds a whip in his hand. Another legendary figure in Chinese history also goes by Zhao Gongming.

增福财神

The fortune god of extra blessings

增福财神，在旧时的北京商家店铺多供奉。实际就是文财神、武财神，或文武财神并坐。红脸者为武财神赵公明，白脸者为文财神比干，并配以各种财神，以及聚宝盆堆元宝，天平秤金锭等。财为五福之一，故进财者增福是也。

In old times, many shops in Beijing offered sacrifices to this god, which is actually the civil fortune god, the military fortune god, or the two sitting side by side. The one with a red face is the military fortune god Zhao Gongming while the one with a white face is the civil god Bi Gan. They are often accompanied by other fortune gods, a treasure bowl, piles of gold and silver ingots, and a scale to weigh the ingots. As wealth is one of the five blessings, where wealth comes in surely blessings are added.

利市三倍

Three times of profit

《周易·说卦》："为近利，市三倍。""利市三倍"意为买卖获利丰厚。旧时的财神像，总配旁利市仙官。利市仙官是民间流传的一位小财神，他是大财神赵公明的徒弟，被姜太公封为迎祥纳福的利市仙官，尤受买卖人欢迎。

The term comes from an ancient Chinese book of the Zhou Dynasty. It means, as it tells, very lucrative business. In old times, the portrait of the gods of fortune was always accompanied by the god of profit. This is a small fortune god popular among the people. A disciple of the master fortune god Zhao Gongming, he was granted the title of god of profit by Jiang Ziya. This figure is a darling for business people.

饮马投钱

Drop coins in the river after watering one's horse

明·程登吉《幼学琼林·文臣》："汉刘宽责民，蒲鞭示辱；项仲山洁己，饮马投钱。"汉朝刘宽仁恕宽厚，为南阳太守时，对有过失的吏民，只用蒲鞭责打。安陵人项仲山，清节不枉取，每饮马渭水，必投钱三枚，清廉之至。

A term to praise those who are clement and upright. A Ming record of recommendable people related that Liu Kuan of the Han Dynasty would reprimand his subjects who had made offences with a whip of cattail, and Xiang Zhongshan would always drop three coins in the river each time he watered his horse.

招财进宝

In comes wealth

《集说诠真》："俗祀之财神，或称北郊祀之回人，或称汉人赵朗，或称元人何五路，或称陈人顾希冯之五子，聚讼纷如，各从所好，或浑称曰财神，不究伊谁。"民间奉祀的财神，多有招财、进宝二位童子，以寓"招财进宝"。

In old China, many gods over fortune were worshipped by different people from the various regions according to their customs and preferences. Sometimes the title "fortune god" was given to all these spirits regardless of their origin and actual identity. Yet fortune gods Zhao Cai and Jin Bao are the more popularly accepted ones as their names suggest wealth.

招财进宝

In comes wealth

《封神演义》第九十九回“姜子牙归国封神”中，曾封陈九公为“招财使者”，肖升为“招财天尊”。后来，“招财进宝”便成了商家求财的神灵名号。此图与下图为旧时商家贴用的“对屏”，分有“进”、“财”两个大字。

In ancient Chinese works of art, there are stories about how Jiang Ziya granted Chen Jiugong and Xiao Sheng titles of officers over wealth, or Zhao Cai. Later on, “In comes wealth” became the magic words businesses use to seek wealth. This picture and the one following are a pair of screens used by merchants of old times. They have the characters Jin and Cai (in comes wealth) respectively.

招财进宝

In comes wealth

两幅图画的均是旧时商家情景。上幅图中有武将打扮，执鞭骑马的南路财神，使人送来装满元宝的聚宝盆。此图中有文官打扮的西路财神，带人推车送来摇钱树。图中还分别有“招财童子”、“公平交易”等字，均表示“招财进宝”。

The two pictures describe the situation of what merchants of past time looked like. In the one above, there is the military fortune god with a whip in his hand on a horse, ordering his people to send over a treasure bowl full of gold ingots. The other picture draws a civil fortune god leading his people to carry over a tree that sheds coins when shaken. Banners that read “fortune gods” and “fair trade” are seen in these pictures.

招財進寳

招财进宝

In comes wealth

招财进宝，自然离不开各路财神的保佑。此图中招财进宝的是五路财神，中间的长者是武财神赵公元帅，其余四位是赵公元帅手下的四位财神：招宝天尊萧什，纳珍天尊曹宝，招财使者陈九公，利市仙官姚少司。推车为民进宝。

To make a fortune depends closely on the protection and blessing of all the fortune gods. The presiding gods in this picture are the five fortune gods – the elderly military fortune god Zhao Gongming sitting in the middle, and the four small fortune gods under him, i.e., Xiao Shen, Cao Bao, Chen Jiugong, and Profit. They are pushing a cart to present treasure and wealth to the people.

招财进宝

In comes wealth

此幅“招财进宝”图为窗画，窗画多流行于河北、山西一带，因北方入冬寒冷，门窗紧闭，每逢年节时换贴窗画于窗格，以点缀节日气氛。窗画一般是四寸正方形或菱形，也有一些更大的窗花。此图以聚宝盆示“招财进宝”。

This is a window picture featuring wealth. Window pictures are popular in Hebei and Shanxi provinces. The climate is cold in winter in North China, and the doors and windows have to be tightly closed. New window pictures are pasted at New Year time and festivals to echo the festive air. These pictures are normally square or diamond of four inches in size though there are also larger window pictures. A treasure bowl is placed on the picture to imply the coming in of wealth.

招财进宝

In comes wealth

此图是以文字为主，图文并茂的吉祥图。“招财进宝”四字，以“钱”图代“财”字，由“进”、“宝”、“招”三字组成一个字，“宝”与“招”置于“进”的走之上，并突出了中间的“宝”字。图中的四只蝙蝠与招财进宝之“财”，组成“五福”。

This is a lucky picture of both copy and visuals. The characters indicating “in comes wealth” are so arranged that they form one large character while featuring the word “treasure ”. The four bats in the picture and “fortune” in the centre – the theme of this picture, form the five blessings.

招财利市

Worshipping the fortune god for great profits

《归安县志》："湖（州）俗好淫祀，有金元六总管、七总管。市井中目为财神，建庙广祝，每月初二、十六日用牲醴，与五圣同饷，名曰拜利市"。金元七总管是旧时江浙一带供奉的财神，本是一位水神，后来成为了财神。

Local records from the lower reaches of the Yangtze River give this account: the region indulged in offering sacrifices to such gods as the sixth and seventh superintendents. The business people saw the seventh superintendent, originally a god of water, as the god of fortune and built temples to worship him. Sacrifices of animals and fish were made to him on the second and 16th of each month to beg for business profits.

招财利市

Worshipping the fortune god for great profits

《乾淳岁时记》：腊月二十四日，市井迎傩，以锣鼓遍至人家乞求利市，“利市”一词由来已久。民间年画多将“利市”画成年轻仙官模样等，称其能引财聚宝。“市”是集中做买卖的场所，也表交易，又示购买，“招财利市”多为商家所用。

The 24th of December of the lunar calendar is the occasion for the marketplace to greet the god of profit. Gongs and drums are beaten along the street, begging for profit from all the households along the way. The word “lishi” (profit) has been used for a long time. It is often painted into a young immortal in New Year pictures and bestowed with the capabilities of bringing wealth. While “shi” (market) is the place where deals are made, the word itself also means transactions and purchase.

招财和合

In comes wealth in harmony

旧时春节，道士常以木刻印制之符箓赠予游寺观或进香祈福者，名曰“旺相”，祝施主岁首新春福寿康宁，借此得到布施。图上画一形如八卦，又似金钱之符箓，两边分刻“樟柳二仙，招财和合”八字。下有和合二仙，外环咒语。

In the past, during the Chinese New Year, Taoist priests would give away wooden printed signs to tourists or worshippers to wish the donators good fortune, health, and peace in the new year in exchange of the donations they get. The picture here has a sign that looks like a coin as well as the Eight Trigrams. Wordings that read "in comes wealth in harmony under the blessings of the two gods of harmony" are engraved on the sides and the two gods are drawn below. The outer circle is a line of incantation.

招财和合

In comes wealth in harmony

此图为道家的符箓，上有道家的八卦图符。和合二仙是民间俗神，清雍正皇帝御封寒山为"和圣"，拾得为"合圣"。《周礼》："使媒求妇，和合二姓。"和合二圣为喜神、爱神，而"招财和合"中的"和合"取意"和气生财"。

This picture is a Taoist sign with the Eight Trigrams. The two gods of harmony, Han Shan and Shi De, are local gods of the people granted by Emperor Yongzheng of the Qing Dynasty. Since the Zhou Dynasty, harmony has been the concern of people in marriages. The two gods of harmony are guardians of love and happiness and harmony here implies that wealth generates from friendly feelings.

金钱虎

Money tiger

满身古钱的金钱虎口衔宝剑，是富贵、威武的象征。并能驱邪除恶，老虎脚下踩着“五毒”。图为清代上海的瑞符，虎身上的古钱除有明、清的“洪武通宝”、“宣统通宝”外，还有日本的“明治通宝”、“宽永通宝”。可见中日吉祥图之交流。

The money tiger has spots of coins all over its body. A sword in the mouth, it is the symbol of wealth and might. Stepping on the “the five poisonous creatures of scorpion, viper, centipede, house lizard and toad”, it has the power to drive away evil. The picture shows a lucky sign from Shanghai in the Qing Dynasty. On the body of the tiger are Chinese coins from the Ming and Qing dynasties as well as Japanese coins with writings indicating the time the coins were minted. This serves to illustrate the extensive exchange of pictures of good omen between China and Japan.

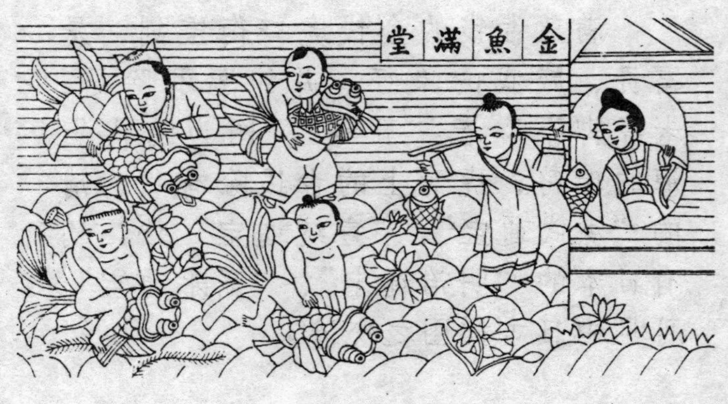

金玉满堂

A full house of gold and jade

《老子》：“金玉满堂，莫之能守。”称誉才学过人。《世说新语·赏誉》：“五长史谓林公：‘真可谓金玉满堂’。”也谓财富极多。优美的鱼形图纹，早在原始社会的陶器上就已出现。以金鱼满池塘，谐音取意满堂都是金玉。

Laozi used the expression “full of gold and jade” to refer to people of extraordinary talents. In other writings, the phrase was deployed to mean a great quantity of wealth. Beautiful fish prints had long ago appeared on pottery of primitive societies. Through the use of a pun, a full pond of goldfish in this picture implies a full house of gold and jade.

金玉满堂

A full house of gold and jade

图中以两条金鱼在池塘中游戏，表示“金玉满堂”。金鱼源于我国，南宋时已开始金鱼家化的研究。金鱼是名贵观赏鱼，被称为“金鳞仙子”、“水中牡丹”等。西方人称之为“东方圣鱼”，现在世界各国的金鱼均源于我国。

Two goldfish swimming in the vat implies a full house of gold and jade. Goldfish originated from China and the study of the domestication of goldfish started from the Song Dynasty. Goldfish is a precious fish for appreciation and has been given such titles as “fairies of gold scales” and “water peonies”, etc. Westerners call it “sacred fish of the orient” as all goldfish of the world originated from China.

鱼吐金钱

Fish producing money in the mouth

这是旧时山东潍县的一幅木刻年画，采用了文图结合的形式。童子怀抱一条金色鲤鱼，即有“余”，又有“金”。而且金鱼又吐出金钱，真是钱财不断，这是人们对“财”的乞盼。“鱼吐金钱”与“连年有余”，有异曲同工之妙也。

This is a woodcut New Year picture of Wei County in Shandong Province from the old times. It has both copy and visuals. The boy holds a goldfish representing both “plenty” and “gold”. As the fish produces money from its mouth, there is an endless source of wealth. This expresses the hope of the people for wealth. “Fish producing money in the mouth” expresses the same idea as “great abundance year after year” through different artistic deliberations.

肥猪拱门

A fat pig knocks the door open

从甲骨文可看出“屋内有豕(猪)”为“家”。可见上古人们的牧业是从养猪开始的，可见猪对人之重要。联：“一夜连双岁，五更分两年。”旧时除夕非常热闹，家家户户都希望新的一年财富不断，即有财神叫门，又有肥猪拱门。

Oracle bones reveal a Chinese home is where there is a pig in the house. As animal husbandry started with pig raising in ancient times, pigs are beyond any doubt animals with significant bearing on people. The couplet in the picture reads "New Year eve connects two years". Chinese New Year eve is a particularly busy and happy time in old times and all households hope that wealth rolls in continuously in the new year. Knocking on the door will be not just pigs but the god of fortune as well.

金驹进宝

The darling horse carries in gold

马日行千里，是古代最快的交通工具。马能驮物，可运输；马能驰骋，可打仗。自古来马就与人有着密切的关系。旧时民间有“宝马驮来千倍利”之说，因此，马在这里也就成了一种财富的象征。吉祥图中常见宝马形象。

The horse was the fastest form of transportation in ancient times. Used in transportation as well as warfare, horses have had a close relationship with mankind since the earliest of times. An old proverb goes “a darling horse brings tons of gold”, associating the horse with a symbol of wealth. The beautiful images of horses are common elements in pictures of good omens.

金驹献宝

The darling horse brings in gold

财富，是老百姓生活的基础，故旧时"进宝"、"献宝"的吉祥图很多，如"推车进宝"、"骆驼进宝"、"招财进宝"、"财神献宝"等等。马，为人类立下了汗马功劳，且多有吉祥之意，故马也称为"宝马"、"金驹"、"龙马"、"龙驹"。

As money is the rudiment of life for people, pictures of old times tend to figure the in-come of money, like "in comes money with a cart", "treasure brought in by a camel", "the god of fortune presents wealth and rank", etc. As the horse makes great contribution to mankind, it is well tied with good omens and auspicious signs. The loyal and capable creature has won such complimentary titles from its grateful master as "darling horse", "gold horse", and "dragon horse".

荣华富贵

Wealth and rank

宋·苏轼《和述古拒霜花》："千林扫作一番黄，只有芙蓉独自芳；唤作拒霜知未称，看来却是最宜霜。"芙蓉花凌霜斗妍，自身就是欣欣向荣的写照。且"蓉"与"荣"谐音，"花"与"华"通假，"牡丹"示"富贵"，合为"荣华富贵"。

Cotton-rose hibiscus blossom in frost; because of such a trait, it is regarded a flower of character, integrity, and prosperity. "Hibiscus" sounds the same as "prosperity", "flower" is also "wealth", and peony indicates wealth and rank. The two flowers join to convey the message of "wealth and rank".

神仙富贵

Wealth and peace under the protection of the immortals

《水仙花赋》："水仙花非花也，幽楚窈眇，脱去埃滓，全如近湘君、湘夫人、离骚大夫与宋玉诸人。"相传水仙为水中仙子所化，以水仙喻神仙。《爱莲说》："牡丹，花之富贵者也。"牡丹示富贵。"神仙富贵"意为神仙保佑，富贵平安。

An ancient Chinese poem on daffodils highly praises the flower for its elegant pose and likens it to ancient Chinese figures of extraordinary integrity. Some say daffodils are the spirits of water fairies. Peony flowers are the symbols of wealth and rank in China. The two flowers together send a wonderful wish for wealth, rank and peace under the protection of immortals.

恭喜发财

Congratulations on your fortune

旧俗逢年过节之时，开张大吉之日，人们见面常以“恭喜发财”相互问候。《荀子·成相》：“务本节用财无极。”民间“五福”为福、禄、寿、喜、财，五福多与财有关，财富是人们生活的物质基础，是人们追求的重要对象。

Under the old customs, on occasions of festivals and shop opening, people would greet each other saying "congratulations on your fortune". The five blessings, good fortune, salary and position, longevity, happiness, and wealth all boil down to some bearing on wealth. Wealth provides a material basis for the life of all man and therefore is much sought after.

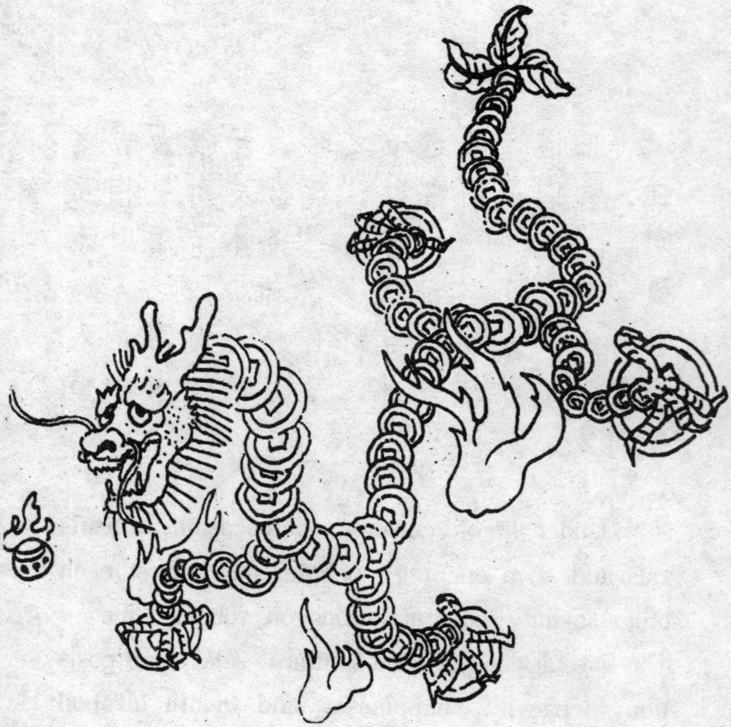

钱龙引进

Fortune introduced by the dragon of coins

铜钱是中国古代的主要货币，铜钱自然是财富的代表。龙是中国古代最大的吉祥物，以铜钱组成的钱龙形象，可以说是富贵吉祥之极。钱龙浑身上下都是钱，并且四爪抓住钱乘祥云而至，引来无数财富。正所谓“钱龙引进四方财”。

Coins were the major currencies in ancient China and naturally the representatives of wealth. The largest animals of good omen, dragon images formed of coins are ultimate expressions of wealth and happiness. The dragon in the picture is clad with coins and comes on auspicious clouds with coins in its claws, bringing a trail of coins along its path.

钱龙引进

Fortune introduced by the dragon of coins

图中引进钱龙的是刘海，金钱顺线而至，组成钱龙。图中也有刘海钓钱之意，民间流传“刘海戏金蟾，步步钓金钱”之语。刘海是钓财散财之神，刘海引进一条条钱龙，然后撒向人间，分发给平民百姓，以保障生活之需。

Liu Hai introduces the dragon of coins in this picture. Coins follow the thread and arrive to form a dragon of coins. Another theme of the picture is that Liu Hai fishes money as there is the proverb "Liu Hai teases the gold toad and fishes money each step he moves". As the god of fortune, Liu Hai introduces one dragon of money after another and disperses all of it among the ordinary people for their living needs.

钱龙引进

Fortune introduced by the dragon of coins

唐高祖李渊于武德四年铸造了一种新颖的钱币“开元通宝”钱，从此在中国货币史上开创了一个崭新的时代，即“通宝”、“元宝”系列钱币时期。图中一童子手执“通宝”钱币做引子，另一童子指钱招手，引来了一条钱龙。

Li Yuan, founder of the Tang Dynasty, minted a novel kind of coins called "kai-yuan-tong-bao" and hence started a brand new epoch in the history of Chinese currencies. In the picture, a boy is holding a coin in his hand as an introduction; another boy is pointing at the coin and beckoning a dragon of coins to come.

钱龙引进

Fortune introduced by the dragon of coins

此图为钱龙聚处，摇钱树上盘着一条口衔金钱金龙，树上结满了无数小的钱龙，一童子在摇钱树上高举“引进钱龙”。既是钱龙聚处，自有财神光临。摇钱树前又有聚宝盆，真是“钱龙引进”，财宝丰收。图中的童子在高兴地收获着钱财。

This picture features the gathering place of money dragons. Wound on the tree of coins is a golden dragon with coins in its mouth; grown on the tree are numerous little dragons of coins. A boy sitting on the tree of coins holds a banner that reads “introduce the money dragon”. Surely the fortune god visits where the dragons of money are gathered. A treasure bowl is situated before the tree of money, a harvest benefited from the dragons of money. Happily another boy in the picture is collecting all the wealth.

得利图

The picture of gains

《本草纲目》："鲤为诸鱼之长，形状可爱，能神变，常飞跃江湖。""鲤"与"利"谐音，图中童子钓得鲤鱼，意为"得利"。"鱼"又与"余"谐音，也示富贵有余。旧时祭财神，多用活鱼，并以红纸蒙鱼眼，以保其鲜活。

Compendium of Material Medical records that the carp is the head of all fish, that lovely in figure, the fish is apt to leap and bound on rivers and lakes. As "carp" and "gains" sound the same in Chinese, the picture of a boy catching a carp equals the picture of gains. As "fish" and "abundance" sounds the same in Chinese, it is at the same time a picture of wealth and abundance. In old times, offerings to the god of fortune are mostly carp with eyes covered in red paper to ensure freshness.

家家得利

Gains to all households

苏轼有句：“享天下之利者，任天下之患；居天下之乐者，同天下之忧。”一人得利，全家欢乐；家家得利，天下太平。图中一身着簑衣的渔夫，从鱼篓中拿出鲜活的鲤鱼，供人挑选购买，以众人买得鲤鱼来表示“家家得利”。

Su Shi, the famous poet of the Song Dynasty said this in his poem: “He who has the gains of this world shoulders the worries and he who enjoys the happiness of this world shares the duties”. One member has gains and the whole family rejoice with him; where all the households have gains, the world is in peace and harmony. In the picture, a fisherman in straw rain cape is offering his fresh catch of carp for selection and purchase by others. The picture sends the message of “gains to all households” through fish purchasing by lots of people.

黄金万两

10 ,000 *ounces of gold*

图中以部首省代法，把“黄金万两”组成一个新的字符。黄金是财富之极，万是数量之极，“黄金万两”表示财富非常多。在中国人的传统观念中，往往把黄金作为最高财富的代表，如“一寸光阴一寸金，寸金难买寸光阴”。

Four Chinese characters, meaning 10, 000 ounces of gold are put together to form a new word. With gold being the ultimate expression of wealth and 10, 000 being the largest number, the phrase stands for a tremendous amount of wealth. In traditional values of the Chinese, gold is often a symbol of an impressive volume of wealth, hence the proverb “So precious is time that it should be measured by gold; yet valuable as gold is, it can not be traded in for time”.

推车进宝

Pushing over the cart to present treasure

《国语·鲁语上》："以其宝来奔。"宝，是玉器的总称，泛指一切珍贵的物品。宝，也是银钱货币，古代的钱币多用"元宝"、"通宝"为文，金银锭也称"元宝"。"宝"是财富的代表，在旧时年画中多有童子推车进宝，以求来年财源滚滚。

A collective word for jadeware, treasure refers to all precious articles, including money, gold, and silver. The word "bao"(treasure) appeared on ancient coins and "yuanbao" stands for gold and silver ingots. In this picture, as in many other New Year pictures of ancient times, a boy is pushing over a cart of treasure, a message and wish for the rolling in of fortune in the coming year.

推车进宝

Pushing over the cart to present treasure

旧时手推小车多为独轮，童子手推一车财宝，均为贵重珍宝，如：火珠、红珊瑚、金元宝等等。旧时，平民百姓连一件珍宝都不可能得到。推车进宝虽是可望而不可及之事，但充分表示了“财”对老百姓的生活是何等的重要。

In old times, hand-pushed carts were mostly one-wheeled, as the one pushed by the boy in the picture. On the cart are treasure goods like flaming balls, red coral, and gold ingots, etc. Ordinary people were not able to possess even a single piece of treasure in old times and "pushing over the cart to present treasure" is but a beautiful dream beyond their reach. But dreams are the best ways to express one's expectations for a good life.

推车进宝

Pushing over the cart to present treasure

《诗经·小雅·何草不黄》："有栈之车，行彼周道。"中国古代即有车——这种在陆地上用轮子转动的交通工具。图有三位童子，一位童子一手抱瓶，一手托元宝，另外两位童子推着满车的财宝。图中还有招财和合保佑。

Carts, transportation tools that moved on wheels on land, started to be used by the Chinese people in ancient times. In the picture are three boys – one holding a bottle (pun for peace) and a gold ingot in the hands, and the other two pushing a cart filled with all kinds of treasures. Lending protection and blessings are the fortune god and the god of harmony.

推车进宝

Pushing over the cart to present treasure

《金陵岁时记》："内容各门亦不一，其制：老年者用推车进宝，四季平安。"旧时有多样"推车进宝"图。此图为四幅连图，四位推车进宝的财神分别是：东路财神、西路财神、南路财神、北路财神，表示财源滚滚四方来。

There were different versions of pictures on the theme "pushing over the cart to present treasure" in old times. Where carts were pushed by elderly people, peace prevailed the whole year round. Here is a running serial of four pictures and the four fortune gods pushing the carts are: fortune god of the east, fortune god of the west, fortune god of the south, and fortune god of the north. As all four directions are covered, the wish is clearly spelled: let wealth come from all corners.

常富贵

Wealth and rank at all times

以铜为镜，可以正冠；以人为镜，可以正己。中国古代的镜子是铜制的，镜的正面光可照人，镜的背面多是精美的吉祥图案或吉祥词语，在这面铜镜的背面示“福”的“蝙蝠”图案，以及“长相思，毋相忘，常富贵，乐未央”之语。

As the mirror serves one to check over his attire, people serve to examine one's own behaviors. Ancient Chinese mirrors were made of bronze with a spotlessly shining front and a back full of beautiful auspicious designs and words of good luck. On the back of this mirror are bat designs that indicate "good fortune" and words that read "always bear affectionate sentiments in the heart and enjoy wealth and stay happy at all times".

累积资金

Capital accumulation

《诗经·周颂·臣工》："庤乃钱镈。"钱，原为古农具名。《国语·周语下》："景王二十一年，将铸大钱。"这里的钱已指铜铸币。图中的招财、进宝二位财神，手捧钱币。只有节流开源，累积资金，才能进一步发大财。

While the Chinese character for money first appeared in the Zhou Dynasty, it originally referred to a farming tool. Two fortune gods, Zhao Cai and Jin Bao, are holding coins in their hands in the picture. As it is the case everywhere, one must control spending and accumulate capital to become further ahead in the list of fortune stars.

添财进喜

Fortune added is happiness increased

财是金钱物资的总称，《荀子》："务本节用财无极。"财是财物，《周礼》："乘其财用之出入。"郑玄注："乘，犹计也；财泉榖也；用，货贿也。"钱财是生活的物质基础，新春伊始，万象更新，家家盼望添财进喜。

As the collective word for money and materials, fortune is the material basis of livelihood and has received the amount of attention it deserves since early human history. At the beginning of the new year and the start of everything, each and every household looks forward to more money and other wealth for the increment of joy in life.

添财进喜

Fortune added is happiness increased

在福、禄、寿、喜、财五福中，往往是福福相连的。洞房花烛夜是人生之大喜，在旧时结婚喜庆时，人们除了贴喜神的吉祥画，同时也贴财神的吉祥画，以图“添财进喜”。图中“囍”字旁坐着文武财神，并有献宝的童子。

The five blessings frequently mentioned by the Chinese, good fortune, salary and position, longevity, happiness, and wealth are often interconnected with each other. At wedding nights, one of the major happy events in life, pictures of good luck featuring both the god of fortune and the god of happiness are pasted to celebrate the occasion. Sitting next to the double happiness word in the picture are the civil and military fortune gods besides boys presenting treasure.

渔翁得利

The fisherman has the gains

《战国策·燕策二》："今者臣来，过易水，蚌方出曝，而鹬啄其肉，蚌合而钳其喙。鹬曰：'今日不雨，明日不雨，即有死蚌。'蚌亦曰：'今日不出，明日不出，即有死鹬。'两者不肯相舍，渔者得而并擒之。"图以"鲤"谐"利"。

A book on the strategies of the Warring States Period records such a story: a clam opened its shell for a sun bathe. A snipe pecked on its flesh and the clam closed its shell. The snipe said that the clam would die after two rainless days and the clam said that the snipe would die also after it got pinched for two days. At this juncture, a fisherman came and caught both of them. The carp in the picture stands for gains.

富贵大吉

Wealth and rank
and extremely good fortune

周敦颐《爱莲说》："牡丹，花之富贵者也。"牡丹花的"富贵花"之名大约始于此。《簪花仕女图》：唐时妇女簪牡丹于髻上，显其妩媚与富贵。"鸡"与"吉"谐音，吉祥图中多以大公鸡喻"大吉"。牡丹花与大公鸡，合为"富贵大吉"之意。

Peony flowers are associated with wealth and rank. Women of the Tang Dynasty wore peony flowers on their coiled bun to show off their charm, wealth and rank. The cock and good fortune are a pun with the same sound in Chinese; so the former appears on the picture to convey the message of latter. The peony flowers and the large cock join to mean wealth and rank and extremely good fortune.

富贵万代

Wealth and rank to thousands of generations

旧联有："积善之家吉祥千载，修福之人富贵万代。"富贵万代喻不仅自己能过好日子、也希望子子孙孙都过着富裕幸福的生活。图以牡丹花示富贵。蔓草，是带状藤蔓植物，"蔓带"与"万代"谐音，合为富贵万代，多出现在传统图案上。

An old couplet reads : "Families exhibiting kindness are fortunate and peaceful to many generations down the line; people aiming at seeking good fortune have wealth and rank to pass on to the 10 ,000th generation". Surely the Chinese people wish their offspring an abundant and happy life, more so than for themselves. Peony here indicates wealth and rank. "Vines" read "thousands of generations" in Chinese, again a pun. So the two combine to mean wealth and rank to thousands of generations. The phrase typically appears on traditional designs.

富贵万年

Wealth and rank for 10 ,000 *years*

富贵万年与富贵万代的意思是一样的。图中富贵花牡丹取其“富”，桂花谐音取其“贵”，万年青取其“万年”，合为“富贵万年”。牡丹花、桂花、万年青，为名贵花种在中国传统文化中都有吉祥之意。寓意为富贵长在，绵延万年。

“Wealth and rank for 10，000 years” means the same as “wealth and rank to thousands of generations”. Three precious plants in the picture, peony flowers, sweet-scented osmanthus, and nandina, are typical representatives of good fortune in Chinese culture. Here they combine to convey the message of lasting wealth and rank.

富贵无极

Endless wealth and rank

富，位列五福，指财丰物饶。贵，地位尊贵，指官高爵显。富贵常合称，因为权势地位与金钱财富往往是共生的，富则贵，贵则富。无极，是无穷无尽之意。富贵无极，指财富之多，地位之高，寿命之长，这都是人们的追求。

Wealth refers to ample money and plentiful of materials. Rank indicates status of high officials in prominent positions. Wealth and rank are often mentioned together as the two are intertwined and connected. Endless wealth and rank is interpreted as extremely wealthy, and extremely high positions and long life, which are the basic pursuits of people.

富贵长春

Wealth, rank, and lasting spring time

宋·周敦颐《爱莲说》：“牡丹，花之富贵者也。”以牡丹花喻富贵。《群芳谱》：月季“一名长春花，一名月月红，一名斗雪红，一名胜春，一名瘦客。灌生，处处皆有，人家多栽插之。”以月季花喻长春。寓春光长在、富贵吉祥。

Peony flowers represent wealth and rank and Chinese roses lasting spring time. An encyclopedia on flowers has this to say about the Chinese rose: the flower has many different names in accordance with its posture and traits, such as monthly red, red in snow, lasting spring, and the slim one, etc. Growing in bushes, the flower is planted everywhere including household gardens and yards. The two flowers combine to indicate lasting spring time and wealth and rank.

富贵平安

Wealth, rank and peace

《管子·治国》："治国常富，而乱国必贫。"国富民强，国泰民安。富贵平安是老百姓的幸福。图以牡丹喻"富贵"，以竹报平安示"平安"，合为"富贵平安"。牡丹为国色天香，竹是"岁寒三友"之一，又是"四君子"之一，均为吉祥之物也。

Ancient Chinese wisdom teaches us that while a well-governed country tends to enjoy wealth, a country in turmoil is doomed to suffer from poverty. Rich countries support a strong populace and peaceful nations see a satisfied people. Wealth and peace translate to happiness on the part of the common people. Peony, symbol of wealth, and bamboo, symbol of peace, join to send the message "wealth and peace" in this picture. Both peony and bamboo are plants of good luck and happiness.

富贵平安

Wealth, rank and peace

牡丹又称富贵花，以示“富贵”。花安插瓶中，以示“平安”。另民俗认为四季桔祝四季平安，与富贵花合为“富贵平安”。周敦颐《爱莲说》：“牡丹，花之富贵者也。”《春秋运斗枢》：“旋星散为桔。”牡丹与桔均为吉祥物。

Peony is also known as the flower of wealth and rank; flowers in a bottle (same pronunciation as peace) indicate peace. Orange is the symbol of good luck and also the symbol of peace throughout the year according to old customs.

富贵有余

Plenty of wealth and high rank

儿童戏鱼，是旧时年画中常见的一种题材。如：连年有余、年年有余、贵子有余、富贵有余、富贵荣华等等。图中一童子怀抱一条鱼，以“鱼”谐音“余”，表示“有余”。莲花又称芙蓉，取“芙”与“富”谐音，表示“富贵”。

Children playing with fish is a common theme seen on Chinese New Year pictures of old times. These include abundance year after year, boys and abundance in the family, and plenty of wealth and high rank, etc. A child in the picture holds a fish (also meaning plenty in Chinese). Lotus flowers share the same pronunciation with "wealth ". Fish and lotus flowers stand for plenty of wealth and high rank.

富贵有余

Plenty of wealth and lasting high rank

《尚书·洪范》："五福：一曰寿，二曰富，三曰康宁，四曰攸好德，五曰考终命。"这里的富指富贵，即财物丰饶，地位尊贵。图以两条金鱼表示"有余"，莲又称芙蓉，表示"富贵"。旧联："富贵有余年年富余，吉庆有祥岁岁吉祥。"

Wealth and rank refer to lots of material goods and prestigious social status. The two goldfish indicate abundance and surplus. Lotus flowers mean wealth and rank. An old couplet from the past reads: "Surplus of wealth and lasting rank, good luck and happiness year after year".

富贵有余

Plenty of wealth and lasting high rank

《太平御览》："君乘金而王，其政讼平，芳桂常生。"《说文解字》："桂，江南之木，百药之长。妇人手中的"桂"谐音"贵"，是象征富贵的吉祥物，童子手中的金驹宝珠也示富贵，童子坐骑金鱼表示"有余"，合为"富贵有余"。

In the picture, the osmanthus the woman holds in her hands and the gold and treasure the child holds symbolize high social rank while the goldfish the child rides on indicates abundance. The visuals serve to send the message of plenty of wealth and lasting high rank.

富贵荣华

Wealth and high rank

唐·李正封诗："国色朝酣酒，天香夜染衣。"唐·皮日休诗："落尽残红始时芳，佳名唤作百花王。"牡丹的"富贵花"名始于《爱莲说》，图以童子手中的牡丹花，示"富贵"。莲花又名芙蓉花，图以"蓉花"表示"荣华"。

Tang poets sang lots of praises to the peony flower : "So astonishingly beautiful is the flower that it resembles drunken beauties in the morning and beats glamorous clothes at night ". The queen of flowers is the title people give to the peony. The beautiful flower held in the hand of the child in the picture represents wealth and rank as in other pictures while lotus flowers symbolize prosperity and high position.

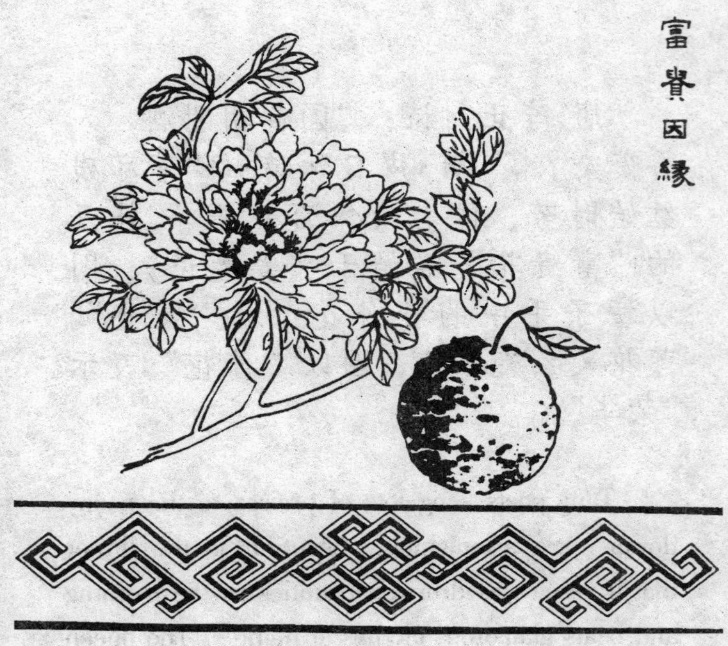

富贵姻缘

Marriage fate of wealth and high rank

清·曹雪芹《红楼梦》第五十七回："自古道：千里姻缘一线牵。"男女结为夫妻是有一定缘分的，故称姻缘。美好的姻缘，自古以来就是人生中的一件大喜事。旧时，常以富贵姻缘表示对新婚的祝福。图以牡丹和圆桔喻之。

Since ancient times, the Chinese regard marriages as arranged by something powerful and irresistible. The fate of marriage brings husband and wife together. Desirable marriages are always great happy events of life. Marriage fate of wealth and high rank is the wish for newly-weds in old China. In the picture here, peony flowers and round oranges serve to convey this message.

富贵童子

Children of wealth and high rank

多子多福，旧时对生子很重视，有贺生子联云："积德累仁自求多福，承先启后生此宁馨。"旧时吉祥画中多有童子形象，人见人爱。图中两位可爱的童子，一位手托金马驹恭进财宝，另一位身背富贵树喜摇金钱，故称"富贵童子"。

In old times, Chinese honored the concept of a lot of children as children are related to good fortune. A couplet celebrating child birth reads: "Seek good fortune through kind deeds and establish good reputation by having children". The image of lovely children is a regular element in old pictures of good luck. In the picture here are two cute children: one is holding a gold horse to present treasure, and the other is carrying a coin tree on the back.

善财童子

Child Shancai

善财童子，是观音菩萨的侍童。据佛经记载，善财是福城长者500个儿子中的小儿子。他出生时，无数财宝从屋中地下涌出，故起名叫善财。善财生财而不爱财，专心修行成佛。民间望文生义，把他当成善于理财、招财的童子。

Child Shancai is the lady's boy of the Goddess of Mercy. According to Buddhist scriptures, Shancai is the youngest son of the 500 sons of Fucheng, a venerable elder. At the time of his birth, numerous articles of treasure rushed to the ground from underneath, and he was therefore named Shancai (kind fortune). Though so named, Shancai devoted his attention not to the collection of wealth but to the studying of Buddhist doctrines. The common folks took him for a fortune god simply on account of his name.

满堂富贵

A household full of wealth

《论语·先进》：“由（仲由）也升堂矣，未入于室也。”古代宫室，前为堂，后为室。《礼记·檀弓上》：“吾见封之若堂者矣。”郑玄注：“堂形四方而高。”在这里堂是指家，“满堂富贵”即家藏万贯之意，与“金玉满堂”意同。

According to ancient Chinese records, the hall and rooms of a house are distinguished based on their functions and shapes. The word “tang” (hall) here refers to the house. Similar to “A full house of gold and jade”, the phrase indicates the family is very rich.

满园堆金

A full garden of gold

元宝形窗外的花园里盛开着金银花，窗下堆着许多古代珍贵的钱币，以示满园堆金。《礼记·儒行》：“儒有不宝金玉，而忠信以为宝。”自古即以金为宝，为财富的代表。财，虽在五福中位居末位，却是生活的物质基础。

Blooming in a flower garden with gold ingot shaped windows are gold and silk flowers; piled beneath the windows are precious ancient coins. This is clearly a picture of a gold garden. While some ancient Confucius scholars treasure not jade and gold but loyalty and faithfulness, gold has since ancient times been the representative of wealth. Wealth, the last of the five blessings, is the material base of daily life.

摇钱树

A tree that sheds coins when shaken

《醒世恒言·卖油郎独占花魁》："只是你的娘，把你当个摇钱树，等闲也不轻放你出去。"摇钱树，是中国古代神话中的宝树，轻轻一摇金钱就掉下来，后用以比喻能挣钱的人。祈盼家家有棵摇钱树，户户有座铸钱炉。

The coin tree, standing for a ready source of income, is the legendary treasure tree in ancient Chinese stories. It refers to people who can generate wealth nowadays. May such a wish be the reality: there is a coin tree in every household and a coin minting machine in each family.

摇 钱 树

A tree that
sheds coins when shaken

此图与下图是一对“门童”画。两幅画上分别有一棵结满钱币的摇钱树，并分别挂一枚大钱币，上面写着“长命富贵”、“金玉满堂”的吉语。两位可爱的童子对称地在树的两旁，从树上一枚一枚地摇摘钱币，表达了人们对钱的需求。

This picture and the one following this form a pair of door boy pictures. On each of the pictures is a tree laden with coins and a large coin is hung on both trees with such auspicious words as “longevity and wealth” and “a full house of gold and jade”. Two lovely children are standing beside each tree picking coins from the trees. The picture expresses the need for money.

摇 钱 树

A tree that sheds coins when shaken

清《天缘记》中，有张四姐点化摇钱树的故事。天女张四姐思凡下界，与贫士崔文瑞成婚，并点化一棵摇钱树，以解生活之需。崔文瑞骤富，邻居王员外起疑，诬崔为盗，崔被捕入狱，后被四姐救出。几经周折，四姐携崔文瑞回天宫。

A Qing story records how Zhang Sijie turned a regular tree into a coin tree. A fairy from heaven, Zhang Sijie came down to the world and got married with a poor fellow Cui Wenrui. To solve the issue of their daily needs, she turned a tree to shed coins. As Cui turned rich from a dubious background, his neighbor ministry councilor Wang charged him of theft and Cui was arrested and put to jail. Zhang Sijie rescued her husband and, after many difficulties, took him back to the heavenly palace with her.

聚宝盆

A treasure bowl

旧时民间有联："摇钱树树摇钱，聚宝盆盆聚宝。"有关"摇钱树"、"聚宝盆"的吉祥画，多以"挂钱"或"窗画"的形式出现。"挂钱"也称"挂笺"、"吊钱""门笺"等，贴于门楣或佛龛上。"窗花"则是贴于窗格之上，点缀节日气氛。

An ancient couplet reads: "As the coin tree sheds money the treasure bowl collects wealth". Pictures of good luck featuring the coin tree and treasure bowl are mostly in the form of door notes on door-heads or Buddhist shrines or window paper-cuts. Pictures of such themes serve to highlight the festive air during festivals and special occasions.

聚宝盆

A treasure bowl

旧时，在表现“聚宝盆”的吉祥画中，往往在盆上都长出一棵摇钱树，一是为画面好看，更是为“盆”、“树”俱有图个财源广茂。而在有关“财”的吉祥图中，也多有“摇钱树”、“聚宝盆”。“摇钱树”只生钱，而“聚宝盆”则百宝俱生。

In old times, good luck pictures featuring the treasure bowl would have a coin tree growing from inside the bowl for a better looking picture. Furthermore, the coin tree and the treasure bowl together would serve as a broader source of fortune. The treasure bowl and the coin tree are common features of propitious pictures. While coins alone are grown on the coin tree, the treasure bowl produces all kinds of precious articles.

图书在版编目（CIP）数据
中华五福吉祥图典.财 / 黄全信主编；李迎春译.—北京：华语教学出版社，2003.1
ISBN 7 - 80052 - 893 - 6
I.中… Ⅱ.①黄… ②李… Ⅲ. 图案 - 中国 - 图集 Ⅳ. J522
中国版本图书馆 CIP 数据核字（2002）第 097608 号

选题策划：单 瑛 英文翻译：李迎春
责任编辑：蔡希勤 封面设计：唐少文
英文编辑：韩 晖 印刷监制：佟汉冬

中华五福吉祥图典—财
主编 黄全信
*

华语教学出版社出版
（中国北京百万庄路 24 号）
邮政编码 100037
电话: 010-68995871 / 68326333
传真: 010-68326333
电子信箱: hyjx @263.net
北京通州次渠印刷厂印刷
中国国际图书贸易总公司海外发行
（中国北京车公庄西路 35 号）
北京邮政信箱第 399 号 邮政编码 100044
新华书店国内发行
2003 年（32 开）第一版
（汉英）
ISBN 7-80052-893 -6 / H · 1429（外）
9－CE－3530P
定价：26.00 元

Printed in China